GOD ^{was} ⁱⁿ this PLACE & I, i ^{did not} ^{know}

GOD ^was ^in
this PLACE
& I, i ^did ^not ^know

Jewish Lights Books by Lawrence Kushner

The Book of Letters: A Mystical Hebrew Alphabet

The Book of Words: Talking Spiritual Life, Living Spiritual Talk

Eyes Remade for Wonder: A Lawrence Kushner Reader

Filling Words with Light:
Hasidic & Mystical Reflections on Jewish Prayer
with Nehemia Polen

God Was in This Place & I, i Did Not Know:
Finding Self, Spirituality and Ultimate Meaning

Honey from the Rock: An Introduction to Jewish Mysticism

I'm God; You're Not: Observations on Organized Religion &
Other Disguises of the Ego

Invisible Lines of Connection: Sacred Stories of the Ordinary

Jewish Spirituality: A Brief Introduction for Christians

The River of Light: Jewish Mystical Awareness

The Way Into Jewish Mystical Tradition

For Children

Because Nothing Looks Like God
with Karen Kushner

The Book of Miracles: A Young Person's Guide
to Jewish Spiritual Awareness

How Does God Make Things Happen?
with Karen Kushner
(SkyLight Paths Publishing)

In God's Hands
with Gary Schmidt

What Does God Look Like?
with Karen Kushner
(SkyLight Paths Publishing)

Where Is God?
with Karen Kushner
(SkyLight Paths Publishing)

Fiction

Kabbalah: A Love Story
(Morgan Road Books)

Jewish Lights 25th Anniversary Edition

GOD was in this PLACE & I, i did not know

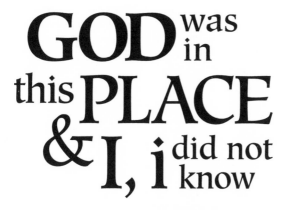

Finding SELF, SPIRITUALITY and ULTIMATE MEANING

LAWRENCE KUSHNER

For People of All Faiths, All Backgrounds

JEWISH LIGHTS Publishing

Woodstock, Vermont

A Note on the Cover

Like lightning, the ladder of Jacob's dream joins heaven and earth. There are seven rungs corresponding to the seven messengers Jacob meets during the night. The colors were chosen in an attempt to evoke the enormous spiritual energy of the dream now visible in the night sky. And their swirling motion was inspired by Vincent Van Gogh's great painting *The Starry Night*.

The reader's attention is directed also to the white diamond shape in the center of the drawing. This is a highly stylized version of the Hebrew letter *yod*, which traditionally represents the Name of God. In addition (as is suggested by the seventh messenger), the letter *yod* is also the first letter of Jacob's Hebrew name, *Yaakov*. In the cover illustration and in the colophon beginning each chapter, this letter *yod* (and Jacob) are suspended midway between heaven and earth, between God and self.

The title of this book, *God Was in This Place & I, i Did Not Know*, is a translation of Genesis 28:16. It is what Jacob says when he awakes after dreaming of a ladder that joins heaven and earth.

God Was in This Place & I, i Did Not Know:
Finding Self, Spirituality, and Ultimate Meaning
Jewish Lights 25th Anniversary Edition

2016 Quality Paperback Edition, First Printing
Copyright © 2016, 1991 by Lawrence Kushner
Cover Art © 2016, 1991 by Lawrence Kushner

Library of Congress Cataloging-in-Publication Data
Names: Kushner, Lawrence, 1943- author.
Title: God was in this place & I, I did not know : finding self, spirituality, and
ultimate meaning / Lawrence Kushner.
Description: Jewish Lights 25th anniversary edition. | Woodstock, VT : Jewish
Lights Publishing, [2016] | Includes bibliographical references.
Identifiers: LCCN 2015050742| ISBN 9781580238519 (pbk.) |
ISBN 9781580238595 (ebook)
Subjects: LCSH: Spiritual life--Judaism. | God (Judaism)--History of doctrines. |
Hasidism. | Bible. Genesis, XXVIII, 16--Criticism, interpretation, etc., Jewish.
Classification: LCC BM723 .K868 2016 | DDC 296.7--dc23 LC record available at
http://lccn.loc.gov/2015050742

10   9   8   7   6   5   4   3   2   1

Manufactured in the United States of America

Book and cover designed and illustrated by the author.

Published by Jewish Lights Publishing
A Division of LongHill Partners, Inc.
Sunset Farm Offices, Route 4, P.O. Box 237 Woodstock, VT 05091
Tel: (802) 457-4000 Fax: (802) 457-4004
www.jewishlights.com

Preface to the 25th Anniversary Edition

"For no thing of the world is set outside the unity of God. But he who does a thing otherwise than toward God separates it from Him."

—BeShT, Martin Buber, *Hasidism & Modern Man*

It's all about who's really Numero Uno. I'll even give you a clue: It's not you. Or, to put it in the syntax of this book's title: There's an uppercase "I" and a lowercase "i" and, despite all your fantasies and plans, you NEVER EVER get to be the uppercase "I." That unique status belongs eternally to the Nameless One. And the book you are holding is about comprehending that essential religious distinction.

The problem—your problem, my problem—is that, even if we concede that we are not the "Uppercase I," we get to thinking that we're running things. It's human nature; everyone does it. Indeed, everything in culture encourages us to think that way. We're in charge. This is our show. We alone are responsible. We know, pretty much, what's going on and we can, pretty much, make most things happen the way we like. It's only when we cannot that we turn to religion. Religion is what you do when you realize you're not God.

But there's more: All the theologies of all the religions agree. There is only one thing to know: Your ego is what stands between you and holiness. The part of you that tells you that you're running things; you're holding both handlebars; you're pulling the strings; you're the boss—that part of you, at least as far as religion is concerned, is the enemy. The bumper sticker should read: "It's your ego, stupid!" Get that sucker out of the way and you stand a fighting chance at meaning and realizing the sacred.

In the words of Talmud tractate Arakin 15b (which always somehow wind up sounding like they're out of a Gary Cooper western), God says, "Ain't room enough in this here world for your ego and Me. You pick." You might say that the Hebrew Bible is a mosaic of stories, laws, and teachings about what happens to people when they get clear about the "Big 'I'" and the "little 'i'," and what happens to them when they get it wrong. This doesn't *mean, of course, that we give up on trying to run our own lives and help all those around us who are likewise trying to run theirs. But it does chasten us to remember that thinking you're able to intercede on behalf of the Holy One, while arguably a benign social convention, leaves little room for holiness.*

As I now review God Was in This Place and I, i Did Not Know *(or as I and Jewish Lights Publishing call it in shorthand, "I, i"), I am chastened to realize how theologically relevant it still seems, twenty-five years after it was first published. Spiritual insights do indeed have very, very brief shelf lives. By their nature, they are dependent on lived experience and refuse to be tamed in words. You live, you learn, you figure it out, but then you realize you must learn it all over again. The spiritual insight must be reexperienced, rediscovered, rehearsed each day. Perhaps that is why we Jews are so patient when it comes to evaluating books.*

LSK

[6]

Acknowledgments

This book grew from a short essay by the late Alexander Altmann of Brandeis University, "God and the Self in Jewish Mysticism," that appeared in Judaism, 1954. The essay was published while he was still a congregational rabbi in Manchester, England. In its few pages he synthesized more than I have been able to assemble in an entire book.

I want to thank Marie Cantlon, my editor, for her confidence, vision, and ability to help me see beyond my own words. The sage counsel and support of friends, especially Anita Diamant, Bill Novak, Nehemia Polen, Jeffrey Summit, and Moshe Waldoks, has been invaluable. The creative enthusiasm of Sandee Brawarsky and Selma Shapiro was also of great help. And I am grateful to the members of congregation BETH EL of the Sudbury River Valley for their understanding and good humor and for permitting me to "field test" so many of the following ideas on them in sermons, classes, and at meetings.

Jevin Eagle's tireless devotion to detail, intellectual energy, and good humor transformed the production of this book into something akin to pleasure. And, of course, without Stuart Matlins, the founder of Jewish Lights Publishing, none of this would have been possible. His advice, trust, and willingness to let me have full graphic control of this book has resulted, I hope the reader will agree, in a seamless blend of aesthetic and literary presentation. He has been mentor, friend, and teacher and made the experience of book-making into one most authors can only dream about.

My children, Noa, Zack, and Lev, have been only blessings throughout the project. The following pages would not have been possible without their continued patience, suggestions, and jokes. Finally, to my wife, Karen: You are my home.

LSK
Sudbury, Massachusetts
7 July 1991
25 Tammuz 5751

To my brother Steven

TABLE *of* CONTENTS

The MIRROR in the ARK

One of a rabbi's happier jobs is making guest appearances in the congregation's pre-school. A few years ago as the High Holy Days approached, their teacher asked if I would give the children a tour of the prayer hall.

I decided to save the contents of the ark, with its ornate, hand-written Torah scrolls of the Five Books of Moses for last. But I lost track of the time and suddenly spied the teacher discreetly signaling from the back of the room that school was almost over, parents soon would be arriving.

Not wanting to rush through the sacred contents of the ark, I decided to save them for a separate session. I apologized for not having enough time and promised the children that the next time we met I would open the curtains and together we would see what was inside. Their teacher later informed me that such a hasty conclusion had generated a heated discussion among the little people as to what exactly was in the ark "behind the curtains."

One kid, doubtless a budding nihilist, thought it was empty. Another, apparently already a devotee of American television consumer culture, opined that behind that curtain was "a brand new car!" Another correctly guessed that it held scrolls of the Torah. But one kid, the teacher insists, said, "You're all wrong. When the rabbi opens that curtain next week, there will just be a big mirror."

אכן יש ה' במקום הזה ואנכי לא ידעתי

PROLOGUE

Surely GOD
was in this PLACE
and I, i did not know
—Genesis 28:16

Like the One who has no mouth, who spoke the first letter that has no sound, the biblical word conceals an infinity of meanings. "She opens a little window in her hidden palace and reveals her face to her lover, then swiftly withdraws, concealing herself." We read the Bible, fix our attention on a phrase, and suddenly find ourselves in a conversation with centuries of teachers who also have come hoping to

Opens a little window
Zohar: The Book of Enlightenment, trans. Daniel Chanan Matt (New York: Paulist Press, 1983), 124.

penetrate the meaning of the same text, convinced that holy words are intimately related not only to what God means but even to who God is and who we are.

The following chapters are about seven different ways of reading the same biblical verse. And while each stands on its own, all reflect on what Jacob says in Genesis 28:16 when he wakes up after having his great dream in the desert about the ladder reaching to heaven with the messengers going up and down. I am amazed to discover the immense amount of disagreement among Jewish teachers over the centuries about what Jacob really meant. In this book these teachers become the "messengers" on the ladder. One by one, they will descend its rungs and try to help Jacob understand what it means to say, "Surely God was in this place and I, i did not know!"

Each teacher's interpretation is clearly supported by the original Hebrew text. Each is coherent, self-contained, and convincing. Jacob may have meant them all, or others still unimagined. We shall never know. Yet, collectively, they represent most, and possibly all, the viable options for understanding the relationship between God's self-concealment and our own self-preoccupation. They also explain Alexander Altmann's elegant dictum that "God is in the self, but the self is not God." For this reason these pages are really, in a larger sense, about one's own self and the Self of the Universe.

Self is not God
Alexander Altmann, "God and the Self in Jewish Mysticism," *Judaism* 3, no. 2 (1954): 146.

Ultimately, all the meanings take on lives of their own. They gather around the ancient table in their several costumes, like wedding guests from distant lands and ancient times. Like ourselves, reverent in the presence of the word that bore them. Meeting one another, sometimes for the first time. Grateful to have been invited. A great banquet of meanings. And it is all there in eight Hebrew words.

ORDINARY FOLKS

A careful reading of the text reveals that the "angels were going up and coming down" on the ladder. The sequence is wrong. If angels reside in heaven, shouldn't the order be the opposite, coming down and going back up? Rabbinic tradition offers several possible explanations.

One suggests that, since Jacob was about to leave the land of Israel, one group of angelic escorts was returning to Heaven and another was descending to watch over him as he began his travels abroad. Another possibility is that the angels symbolized the nations of the world, whose power ascends and descends during the course of history. And still a different interpretation proposes that the angels were not ascending and descending the ladder but were exalting and degrading Jacob going up and down, as it were, "on him."

His travels abroad
Midrash *Genesis Rabba* 68.12.

The course of history
Midrash *Leviticus Rabba* 29.2.

Up and down on him
Midrash *Genesis Rabba* 68.12.

But there is another, even more obvious interpretation. The angels did not reside in heaven at all. They lived on earth. They were ordinary human beings. And, like ordinary human beings, they shuttled back and forth between heaven and earth. The trick is to remember, after you descend, what you understood when you were high on the ladder.

WHO'S on FIRST?

The reason we have such a difficult time speaking of God is not God's fault; the syntax of our language is the culprit. In one of the great comedy routines of all time, Bud Abbott tries to tell Lou Costello the names of the players on the baseball team. Unfortunately for Costello, the names of the players are either not names or are themselves questions. "I dunno" is on third base. "What?" is on second. And, of course, "Who?" is on first.

"That's what I'm trying to find out." asks Costello. "Who's on first?"

"Absolutely," answers Abbott.

"Who?" says Costello.

"Yes," says Abbott.

"Look," shouts Costello in exasperation. "At the end of the week, when you pay the first baseman, who gets the money?"

"Every dollar of it, and why not? The man's entitled to it; he earned it," answers Abbott.

And so it goes. The reason Costello cannot get the answer to his question is that the question is itself the answer. The inability of one who asks to receive the answer is a stubborn insistence on looking for it somewhere else. You already have what you are looking for.

Gershom Scholem, the master historian of Jewish mysticism who is not customarily on stage with American standup comedians, nevertheless expressed a similar idea. He once told me that the ultimate question one can ask, standing at the outer edge of the Kabbalistic seventh *sefirah* (that is, the furthest possible extent of human awareness), is not "What is the meaning of life?" or even "Why am I here?" but simply "Who?" Like all questions, its syntax predetermines the range of possible answers. And the question "Who?" is a request for either a name or a personal pronoun. The answer, in other words, must be personal. It must be a self.

Like the Zen monk who, after years of study, formulated what he thought was the ultimate question—Who am I?—only to be surprised by the voice inside him that replied, "Who is asking?" You are looking for the one who is looking. In this sense, then, this tale is not so much a literary fantasy about the possible meanings of a biblical verse recorded centuries ago, but a journey into the "self" who is reading these words.

READING BETWEEN the WORDS

This book is actually one long midrash, that is, fiction concealed beneath the apparent text of the biblical narrative: what might have happened before and after, above and below the biblical story. Imagine, for instance, that your life, as it superficially appears to others, is the apparent text. Beneath and within you move forces and fantasies—often concealed from those watching and even from yourself—that are the matrix for each outward event. In a similar way, midrash attempts to "imagine" how the apparently discordant "words" of the text might be woven into a larger coherent whole. Such an approach is more than literary criticism. Only when the words of the text are holy or, like a love letter, are read with a diligence of attention bordering on reverence, can midrash occur.

Professor Susan Handelman suggests that a primary difference between Judaism and Christianity springs from the diverging ways the rabbis and the Greeks read words. For the Greeks, and their classical Christian successors, words—like everything else in this world—are only imperfect representations of some higher reality. Therefore for them the goal is to bring what is truly real above down here below. In such

Rabbis and the Greeks
Susan A. Handelman, *The Slayers of Moses: The Emergence of Rabbinic Tradition in Modern Literary Theory* (Albany: State University of New York Press, 1982).

[17]

a universe the central religious act is incarnation: the word made real.

The Hebrew word *dvar*
Ibid., 32.

For the rabbis, on the other hand, the Hebrew word *dvar* means "thing" as well as "word." Words "create, characterize and sustain reality." Primary reality is linguistic. And the biblical word is not only a token of God's unending covenant love, it is also "the real thing." For Jews the central religious act is not incarnation but interpretation. Jewish spirituality begins and, finally, ends with the words of scripture. Michael Fishbane, Professor of Bible at the University of Chicago, once suggested to me that through interpreting the Bible, Jews create themselves over and over again.

The words of Torah
Midrash *Exodus Rabba* 5.9.

Shatters the rock
Jeremiah 23:29; Midrash *Makita De-Rabbi Ishmael*, trans. Jacob Z. Lauterbach (Philadelphia: Jewish Publication Society, 1933), 2:252.

The words of Torah are infinitely analyzable and strike each recipient in a way appropriate to his or her strength and life situation. (This may also explain why arguing plays such a prominent role in Jewish conversation.) Biblical words shatter and rearrange themselves before our sustained gaze. As we read in Jeremiah, "My word is like fire, says the Lord, and like a hammer that shatters the rock."

Single living organism
Gershom Scholem, *Major Trends in Jewish Mysticism* (New York: Schocken, 1941), 14.

Uninterruptable Name
Gershom Scholem, *On the Kabbalah and Its Symbolism*, trans. Ralph Manheim (New York: Schocken, 1965), 39.

The words of Torah are holy because they provide a glimpse into the infrastructure of being. They comprise a single "living organism animated by a secret life which streams and pulsates below the crust of its literal meaning." Midrash tries to imagine ever larger systems of interdependence and meaning. Someday, according to Jewish mystical, or Kabbalistic, tradition, the entire Torah will be read as one long, uninterruptable Name of God. And that, of course, would dissolve not only the boundaries between the words of the text, but also the boundaries separating reader from text, creating the ultimate midrash. Here is the biblical story.

GENESIS 28:10–16

Jacob set out from Beersheba heading toward Haran. He came upon a certain place and, since the sun had set, he spent the night there. He took one of the stones from the place, put it under his head, and lay down there in that place. He dreamed.

And behold: a ladder, standing on earth, its top reaching the heavens. And behold: messengers of God, going up and going down on it. And behold: God is standing on it and says, "I am *Adonai*, the God of Abraham, your father, and the God of Isaac. The land on which you lie, I will give to you and to your progeny. Your descendants shall be as the dust of the earth; and you shall spread to the west and to the east, to the north and to the south; and all the families of the earth shall bless themselves through your descendants. And behold: I am with you, and I will take care of you wherever you go, and I will bring you back to this land, for I will not leave you until I have done as I have spoken."

And Jacob awoke from his sleep and said, "Surely God was in this place and I, i did not know!"

DRAMATIS PERSONAE

Jacob's words sound simple enough. A man lies down in what he takes to be a God-forsaken place and unexpectedly has one of the great visions of the Hebrew Bible. The next morning he says what any normal person might say after such an encounter. Indeed, his words are so reasonable that, were it not for the sustained attention of generations of teachers from second-century Palestine to eighteenth-century Russia, we might even ignore them. Real human beings who ate breakfast, caught colds, and had to earn a living, they all shared the biblical text and therefore (in some mysterious way, I believe) a conversation with Jacob that has been faithfully handed down to us.

This transmission of interpretations from one generation to another is very important in Judaism. The tradition has fashioned rituals designed to preserve not only accuracy but also the identity of the teacher. Insights into the text are taught, *b'shaym omro*, in someone's name. And we are advised to pause for a moment before speaking a teacher's words, so that we may recall his face before our eyes or the sound of her voice in our ear. In this way the teaching comes from someone who, by our deliberate act of memory, continues to live.

For this reason, I also have tried to envision faces and personalities for many of these long-dead teachers. Where ever possible I have constructed them from the fragments of extant sources and, as is often the case, when little or nothing was available, I have made a reverent guess. Indeed, for most of the "characters," there is more fantasy than fact. This artifice is, however, more than an aesthetic choice. In setting the following pages within the imagined lives of real teachers, I hope to reclaim a mode of Jewish writing familiar to any student of midrash, the *Zohar*, or Hasidic legend. And, while this book obviously can never hope to exhibit the same degree of depth and nuance as such classic spiritual texts, like them it is meant to be read slowly.

[20]

Finally, while virtually all of the teachers I have quoted wrote in traditional sexist God language and metaphor, I have assumed they did so out of convention and not from theological conviction about God's masculinity. In the interests of consistency therefore I have modified their words in the same way I would make any minor corrections in syntax, grammar, and spelling. This is especially important since so much of spirituality originates from the feminine side of even male consciousness.

The first "messenger on the ladder" is a man named Rashi. He says Jacob was talking about what it means to be awake.

אכן יש ה' במקום הזה ואנכי לא ידעתי

If I had known God was here,
I wouldn't have gone to sleep

1 / RASHI

AWARENESS

The Hebrew word for angel, *malach*, also means messenger. Sometimes the messengers are ethereal and translucent; other times they are ordinary human beings. Rabbinic tradition views the angelic ones with suspicion. They are often portrayed as jealous of their younger human siblings. One midrash tells how they tried to dissuade God from making people. Another legend observes that while angels stand still, human beings, curious and unsure, ever move along. If

Rashi
Troyes, France
1040–1105.

Tried to dissuade God
Midrash
Genesis Rabba
8.5.

[23]

Static truth
Aharon Yaakov
Greenberg, ed.,
Itturay Torah
(Tel Aviv:
Yavneh Pub-
lishing, 1976),
4:154–55
(Hebrew).

you are suspicious of static truth, better to put your trust in human angels.

One of these messengers "going up and coming down" on the ladder was born in the middle of the eleventh century, in the northern French city of Troyes; his name was Rabbi Shelomo ben Yitzhaki. He is better known by the acronym formed from the initials of his name, Rashi. He wrote such a concise commentary about the literal meaning of the words in the Five Books of Moses that it was the first Hebrew book to be printed mechanically, even before the Bible. Indeed, Rashi's *payroosh*, or commentary, is so clear and so accessible that for centuries it appeared routinely on the same page as the biblical text itself.

**Even before
the Bible**
Edward L.
Greenstein,
"Medieval
Bible Com-
mentaries,"
in *Back to the
Sources: Read-
ing the Classic
Jewish Texts*,
ed. Barry W.
Holtz (New
York: Summit
Books, 1984),
228.

Rashi's impact on the Jewish understanding of scripture is enormous. For more than a millennium, Jewish school children have read the Torah through Rashi's eyes. This is the first step, so it is only sensible to begin our inquiry with Rashi's commentary.

He was a thorough man with (I imagine) a thick crop of brushed black hair, a humble and relentless pedant. Like his life work, everything was straightforward. And while he may not have been much fun at dinner parties, to study in his class must have been thrilling. From Rashi you learned how to do again what you hadn't done since you were a small child: pay close attention to the obvious.

"When you look closely and for a long time, you discover things that are invisible to others. Most people make the mistake of trying to 'look deeper' when all they need is to pay attention to the obvious. Ask yourself, What are the words? What is their order? Review, again and again, the simple elements of the story. Then you will understand." Rashi stopped to relight his pipe.

"All right," answered Jacob. "My story is that I'm running away from a very strange family."

"To call them 'strange' is already an attempt to sound psychologically sophisticated. Let the words of the story speak for themselves."

"I am running away from my family and I went to sleep."

"Better. And who is the story about?"

"It's about me."

"Excellent. The story is literally the text of your life. You need not try to be profound. When you examine it closely, you will discover yourself and all the profundity you need."

The eastern sky was already bright orange with sunrise; Jacob could begin to see the purple shapes of the mountains on the horizon.

ADDRESSED PERSONALLY

There is an old Hasidic story, recounted by Martin Buber, of the disciples who gathered to learn from their *rebbe*, the Baal Shem Tov. After the evening prayers, the master would go to his room where candles would be lit and "the mysterious Book of Creation" lay open on the table. All those seeking advice from the Baal Shem were then admitted in a group to hear their teacher, who would speak late into the night.

One evening as the students left the room, one apologized to the others for monopolizing so much of the Baal Shem's attention. Throughout the entire audience, the master had spoken to him personally. His friend told him not to talk such nonsense. They had all entered the room together and, from the very beginning, the master had spoken only to him. A third, hearing this, laughed and said that they both were mistaken, for their teacher had carried on an intimate conversation with him alone for the entire evening. A fourth and a fifth made the same claim—that the Baal Shem had spoken to them personally, to the exclusion of everyone else. Only then did they realize what had happened, and all fell silent.

So it is with us when we read scripture. The biblical text speaks intimately and demands an intensely personal response. As Harold Bloom has said of reading "strong poetry," the interpretation evoked "insist[s] upon itself ... it and the text are one." Because the words of the poem speak only to me, I am not free to comment dispassionately on them, for I am in them. They are me. What you say of the poem, you say of me.

All fell silent
Martin Buber, *Tales of the Hasidim: The Early Masters*, trans. Olga Marx (New York: Schocken, 1947), 55.

The text are one
Harold Bloom, *Kabbalah and Criticism* (New York: Continuum, 1983), 125.

FIRE WITHOUT FLAME

There is a similar intensity of attention when Moses encounters God at the bush.

> Moses was tending the flock ... beyond the wilderness and he came to the mountain of God, Horeb. An angel of the Lord appeared to him in the heart of a flame from inside a bush. And he looked and behold the bush burned in fire yet the bush was not consumed. Moses said, "I must turn aside now so that I can see this awesome sight: Why is the bush not consumed." When the Lord saw that he had turned aside to look, God called to him from within the bush.

From within the bush
Exodus 3:1–4.

[26]

The story is customarily offered as a "miracle" that God performed to get Moses' attention. This fails to explain why God, who could split the sea, fashion pillars of fire, and make the sun stand still would resort to something so trivial and undramatic to attract Moses' attention as to make a bush burn without being consumed. It is a cheap trick.

Look more closely at the process of combustion. How long would you have to watch wood burn before you could know whether or not it actually was being consumed? Even dry kindling wood is not burned up for several minutes. This then would mean that Moses would have had to watch the "amazing sight" closely for several minutes before he could possibly know there even was a miracle to watch! (The producers of television commercials, who have a lot invested in knowing the span of human visual attention, seem to agree that one minute is our outer limit.)

The "burning bush" was not a miracle. It was a test. God wanted to find out whether or not Moses could pay attention to something for more than a few minutes. When Moses did, God spoke. The trick is to pay attention to what is going on around you long enough to behold the miracle without falling asleep. There is another world, right here within this one, whenever we pay attention.

SIMPLE READINGS

Jacob was waking up. Confused by the wilderness in which he found himself, shaken by the dream's power, and frightened by the message, he wipes the thickness from his eyes and whispers, "Wow! God really must have been right here, in this place, and I, i did not know!"

Gone to sleep
The source of all ritual impurity is death. Thus anything that might have made life but did not, such as menstrual blood or semen, is ritually defiling. At Sinai the people of Israel may have remained awake all night and kept distant from the opposite sex as a precaution against inadvertently becoming impure. Rashi's comment also reflects his own traditional concern with purity. Had Jacob known it was a holy place, he would have remained awake all night. For moderns, awareness may be all that remains of ritual purity.

Commentary on Rashi's commentary
Shabbetai ben Joseph Bass, *Siftei Chachamim* (Frankfort on Main, 1712). An anthology of other supercommentaries.

Rashi's comment, as it appears beneath the boldfaced, over-sized Hebrew text of the traditional *Mikraot Gedolot*, or study Bible, demonstrates the power of paying meticulous attention to the words before us. What Jacob means is so obvious, it is almost comical, says Rashi: "If I had known [that God would have been here], I wouldn't have gone to sleep in such a holy place!" Or, as the commentary on Rashi's commentary, *Siftei Chachamim*, explains, we may assume that Jacob said what he said because he must have learned something about being asleep. "Otherwise ... what difference would it make to him if he didn't know [that God had been there]?"

The beginning of knowing about God, in other words, is simply paying attention, being fully present where you are, or as Rashi suggests, waking up. We realize, like Jacob, that we have been asleep. We do not see what is happening all around us. For most of us, most of the time, the lights are on but nobody's home.

Right now, for instance, you are a reader. You are consuming these words and the ideas they bear. But suppose you were a typographer, then you would also notice the shapes of the letters. Suppose you were a poet. A paper manufacturer. A blind person. A composer. We find what we seek. And we seek who we are.

OBLIVIOUS to MIRACLES

Jewish tradition says that the splitting of the Red Sea was the greatest miracle ever performed. It was so extraordinary that on that day even a common servant beheld more than all the miracles beheld by Isaiah, Jeremiah, and Ezekiel combined. And yet we have one midrash that mentions

[28]

two Israelites, Reuven and Shimon, who had a different experience.

Apparently the bottom of the sea, though safe to walk on, was not completely dry but a little muddy, like a beach at low tide. Reuven stepped into it and curled his lip. "What is this muck?"

Shimon scowled, "There's mud all over the place!"

"This is just like the slime pits of Egypt!" replied Reuven.

"What's the difference?" complained Shimon. "Mud here, mud there; it's all the same."

And so it went for the two of them, grumbling all the way across the bottom of the sea. And, because they never once looked up, they never understood why on the distant shore everyone else was singing songs of praise. For Reuven and Shimon the miracle never happened.

Call it the difference between epistemology and piety. In epistemology if a tree falls in the forest and no one is there to hear, it may or may not make a sound. In piety if a miracle happens and no one notices, it did not happen. Each miracle requires at least one person to experience the miracle, even if, like Jacob, only in retrospect.

> **The miracle never happened**
> Midrash *Exodus Rabba* 24.1.

Now Jacob begins to ponder the events of his life in a new way. A dimension of what has come to be called "the spiritual" now lies open. "If God was here, and I didn't know, then perhaps God has been other places also."

JEWISH SPIRITUALITY?

Classical Hebrew has no word for spirituality. (The modern Hebrew, *ruchaniyut*, comes from our English word.) The English word "spiritual" means immaterial and connotes the religious. The concept comes to us with the heavy baggage of early Christianity that divides the universe into material and spiritual. This tradition teaches how to leave this gross, material world and get to the other real, spiritual, and, therefore, holy one.

Judaism sees only one world, which is material and spiritual at the same time. The material world is always potentially spiritual. For Judaism all things—including, and especially, such apparently non-spiritual and grossly material things as garbage, sweat, dirt, and bushes—are not impediments to but dimensions of spirituality. To paraphrase the Psalmist, **Full of God** "The whole world is full of God." The business of religion is **Psalm 24:1.** to keep that awesome truth ever before us.

Spirituality is that dimension of living in which we are aware of God's presence. "It is being concerned with," in the words of Martin Strelser, "how what we do affects God and how what God does affects us." It is an ever-present possibility for each individual. Jewish spirituality is about the immediacy of God's presence everywhere. It is about patience and paying attention, about seeing, feeling, and hearing things that only a moment ago were inaccessible.

INAUDIBLE SCREAMS

I once knew a man who was in psychoanalysis. His doctor's office was across the street from an old, red-brick, inner-city psychiatric hospital. One day, as he had regularly done for a few years, my friend walked down the street to his car in front of the hospital. Suddenly he heard a blood-chilling scream from the top floor that seemed to sound the deepest pain a soul could possibly feel. This unforgettable noise etched itself into his soul. The following day, back on the couch, he told his doctor of the scream from the top floor. To his astonishment, his therapist was surprised that he should mention it at all.

"You mean you just now heard it?" asked the doctor. "After all these years? On the top floor across the street, that's where they put all the screamers." And from that day on, my friend said, he was able to hear the screams on the top floor almost every time. "The screams are all around us," he later mused, "waiting for our ears and eyes and hands."

ULTIMATE AWARENESS

Aldous Huxley, paraphrasing Henri Bergson, once suggested that we are potentially able to be aware of everything.

> Each person is at each moment capable of remembering all that has ever happened to him or her and of perceiving everything that is happening everywhere in the universe. The function of the brain and nervous system is to protect us from being overwhelmed and confused by this mass of largely useless and irrelevant knowledge, by shutting out most of what we should otherwise perceive or remember at any moment, and leaving only that very small and special selection which is likely to be practically useful.

Aware of everything Aldous Huxley, *The Doors of Perception* (New York: Harper & Row, 1954), 22–23.

Universal consciousness is too much to handle and would burn out the circuitry. In Thoreau's words, "I have never yet met a man who was quite awake. How could I have looked him in the face?" We must therefore create an elaborate system of filters, lenses, and blinders to screen out the extraneous images, leaving us with a very small field of vision. What we call consciousness is all that remains visible

Looked him in the face Henry David Thoreau, *Walden and Other Writings*, ed. Brooks Atkinson (New York: Random House, 1937), 81.

[31]

in this tiny patch of the light of our attention. We can aim it at anything we like, but only a very few things at a time. How we will focus and direct the beam is up to us.

BACKGROUND MUZAK

Classic religious terms
Eliyahu KiTov, *Sefer HaParshiyot* (Jerusalem: Aleph Publishers, 1965), *Parashat Terumah*, 128 (Hebrew).

Voice issues from Sinai
Mishna tractate *Avot* 6.2.

Eliyahu KiTov, the Orthodox Israeli commentator, poses this problem in classic religious terms. We know that the Torah was given once and for all time at Sinai. Yet the Torah's words are so important that our sages say, "Each and every day the Divine Voice issues from Sinai."

Not only then is Torah eternally unchanging, it is also always present, always able to be heard. Right here and right now, the Holy One of Being is saying the very same words that were said at Sinai. This poses two problems: If Torah is being spoken all the time, then why can't we hear it? And, if Torah is being spoken all the time, what is so special about the revelation at Sinai? KiTov answers both questions with a daring insight into the nature of consciousness.

The reason Sinai is so special and the reason why we are unable to hear Torah all the time, he suggests, is because the noise, static, and muzak of this world drown out the sound of God's voice. Only at the time of the "giving of the Torah" did God "silence the roar." In the language of modern sound-recording technology, God, you might say, switched on the "Dolby" noise reduction system. At Sinai we could hear what had been there (and continues to be here) all along.

God is the One who enables us to hear what is being spoken at the most primary levels of reality. Each act of conscious focus is a miniature Sinai that now can be in every place.

This VERY PLACE

In rabbinic tradition, the Hebrew word for "place," *makom*, is also a name for God. This occasions some fascinating word plays. According to the Midrash,

> [When] the brothers of Joseph saw that their father was dead ... they were afraid. They saw that at the time they were returning from burying their father, Joseph went to offer a blessing at that pit into which [they] ... had thrown him. And he offered a blessing over it, as one is obligated to do at a place where a miracle has been done for him: "Blessed be the *makom* [the Place? God?] who made a miracle for me in this place."

Miracle for me
Midrash *Tanhuma* ver. A, *Vayechi* 17, end.

Likewise, in our story of Jacob's dream, we read that he "came upon the place/*makom*." One midrash, punning on the word *makom*, suggests that it means that Jacob came upon God! Another midrash cites a teaching of Rabbi Huna, who taught in the name of Rabbi Ammi, and makes the misreading into theology:

Jacob came upon God
Midrash *Pirke deRabbi Eliezer*, ch. 35.

> Why do we change the name of the Holy One, and call God *makom* [the Place]? Because God is the place of the world and not the other way around. Rabbi Jose bar Halafta said: We do not know whether God is the place of the world or whether the world is God's place, but from the verse, "Behold, there is a place with Me," it follows that the Lord is the place of the world, but this world is not God's place.

Place with me
Exodus 33:21.

Not God's place
Midrash *Genesis Rabba* 68.9; Ephraim E. Urbach, *The Sages: Their Concepts and Beliefs*, trans. Israel Abrahams (Jerusalem: Magnes Press, 1975), 68–72.

God, the Holy One of Being, is more than everywhere; God is the bosom in which creation happens day after day, the ground and the source of everything that exists, the very

Place of Being itself
"Why is the name of the Holy One called *makom*? Because ... as it is said, 'In every place where I record my name I will come unto you and bless you.'" Exodus 20:24, Midrash *Pirke deRabbi Eliezer*, ch. 35.

There is a place Exodus 33:21

Place of Being itself. And to be awake and present "in this place" is to encounter God. In Rashi's words, as he comments on the verse in Exodus, "On the mountain where I speak with you always, there is a place prepared by Me for your sake where I will hide you so that you will not be injured. From there you will see what you will be permitted to see. This is its simple meaning."

Jacob lay there remembering his father Isaac, and his grandfather Abraham, and the terrible mountain they called Moriah—"the place where God will be seen." According to one rabbinic legend, it was in this same ubiquitous place, unbeknownst to Jacob, that he had just had his dream.

BEING PRESENT

You already are where you need to be. You need go nowhere else. Feel it now in the moisture on your tongue. Sense the effortless filling and emptying of your lungs, the involuntary blinking of your eyes. Just an inch or so behind your sternum where your heart beats. That is where the *makom* is. Right here all along and we did not know it because we were fast asleep, here in this very *makom*.

In each created thing Menahem Nahum of Chernobyl, *Upright Practices: The Light of the Eyes*, trans. Arthur Green (New York: Paulist Press, 1982), 100.

Awaken the holiness *Itturay Torah*, 2:248.

In the panentheism of the Hasidic revival, as Rabbi Menachem Nahum of Chernobyl taught, "All being itself is derived from God and the presence of the Creator is in each created thing." Or in the words of Rabbi Aryeh Lieb of Ger, "A person is able to awaken the holiness of God in any place."

Rabbi Menachem Mendl of Kotzk (who is on the ladder just behind Rashi) observed that the verse in Exodus seems to be redundant. God says to Moses, "Come up to Me on

[34]

the mountain and be there." If Moses were to ascend the mountain, why would God also bother to specify that he "be there"? Where else would he be? The answer, suggests the Kotzker, is that people often expend great effort in climbing a mountain, but once they get there, they're not there; they're somewhere else.

And be there
Exodus 24:12.

Somewhere else
Itturay Torah, 3:199.

Jacob looked at Rashi. Years of being a teacher had taught the older man that the most powerful moments of teaching occur when the teacher has enough self-control to remain silent. The slightest noise, even a gesture could ruin everything. Jacob was waking up.

אכן יש ה' במקום הזה ואנכי לא ידעתי

*God was here because I was able to
subdue my ego*

2 / KOTZK

EGOTISM

Rashi sought the truth through a meticulous, literal reading of text and life experience; Menachem Mendl of Kotzk sought the truth through stripping away the ego. It was an uncompromising, harsh, even fanatical pursuit. "All I want," declared Menachem Mendl, "is that ten Jews stand on the rooftops and cry out 'The Lord is God!'" The religious energy of Menachem Mendl's school was so focused and intense that it bordered on madness. Indeed, for the last twenty

Menachem Mendl of Kotzk Kotzk, Poland, 1787–1859.

On the rooftops Abraham Joshua Heschel, *Passion for Truth* (New York: Farrar, Straus & Giroux, 1973), 36, 309.

years of his life, the Kotzker lived in virtual self-isolation. To this day among the Hasidim if a student's obsession with finding truth makes him a social nuisance, he is told, "Go live in Kotzk!"

The school of Kotzk was a revolution within the great eighteenth-century Jewish spiritual revolution of Eastern Europe. Hasidism, as it came to be known, began as a reaction against the Talmudic aridity and social stratification of the times. Centuries of refining the most rigorous patterns of study by which students learned to rehearse complicated and often arcane arguments over Jewish religious and civil law increasingly left little room for non-linear thought. The brightest students also married into the wealthiest families, further narrowing the top of the social pyramid. Hasidism offered an alternative.

Through religious fervor and the mediation of one's spiritual master or *rebbe,* the Hasidic movement returned religious power to the masses, kindling a revival that continues to this day. Hasidism was founded by Israel Baal Shem Tov or, as he is more commonly known by his initials, simply the *Besht.* Whereas the Hasidism of the Baal Shem was populist and kind, in Kotzk the fervor was elitist and harsh. In Abraham Joshua Heschel's words, "In Medzibosh [the home of the Baal Shem] there was light—in Kotzk fire." The Besht emphasized love, joy, and compassion. "Kotzk demanded constant tension and an unmitigated militancy in combating ... egocentricity."

Unmitigated militancy
Encyclopedia Judaica, s. v. "Menachem Mendel of Kotzk."

The Talmud says: "When Nebuchadnezzar, the mighty King of Babylonia, wanted to sing praises to God, an angel came and slapped him in the face." Asked the Kotzker, "Why did he deserve to be slapped if his intention was to sing God's praises?" He answered himself: "You want to sing praises while you are wearing your crown? Let me hear how you praise me after having been slapped in the face."

The students who gathered in Kotzk were slapped in the face. They understood the injury as a necessary step toward apprehending the truth. And each day the truth had to be "found anew, as if it had never been known." In this search, their constant and greatest adversary was none other than their own egos. "The true worship of God ... is not in finding the truth, but rather in ... total abandonment of self."

Slapped in the face
Passion for Truth, 191.

Truth had to be found
Encyclopedia Judaica, s. v. "Kotzk."

Abandonment of self
Encyclopedia Judaica, s. v. "Kotzk."

A COLD WHITE FLAME

From the way his body moved, it was a miracle that Menachem Mendl could descend the ladder. He was (I imagine) overweight and bony at the same time, as if the inside of the body was not intended for the outside. This gave him the overall appearance of a lobster, a lobster with a scruffy beard who glared back at you through dark and recessed eyes.

His laugh was nurturing, contagious, and utterly disarming. That was how he caught you. He would say very funny, even coarse things and laugh. Then you would laugh. And you were his forever. Not until much later when you were warming yourself would you be frightened by the cold white fire burning in his soul. You came expecting to be sternly judged, instead you wound up laughing. Things you thought were humorous, the Kotzker thought were hilarious. It was so gratifying to be witty and clever for him, then when you said something less than the truth he would scream at you and make you want to cry and beg for just a word of comfort. Occasionally, a few minutes later, he would return and yell some more.

Ever seen a wolf
Martin Buber,
Tales of the Hasidim: The Later Masters, trans. Olga Marx (New York: Schocken, 1948), 279.

"Have you ever seen a wolf?" the rabbi of Kotzk asked one of his Hasidim.

"Yes," he replied.

"And were you afraid of him?"

"Yes."

"But were you aware of the fact that you were afraid?"

"No," answered the hasid. "I was simply afraid."

"That is how it should be with us when we fear God."

OPPOSITION to the EGO

Some meeting this is: Menachem Mendl of Kotzk and Jacob. A fanatic for attaining truth through negating the ego meets the Hebrew Bible's paradigmatic egotist. Of all the messengers on the ladder, the Kotzker most closely resembled Jacob. Both are preoccupied with self.

By the time Menachem Mendl came down the ladder, Jacob was deep into one of those mental self-examinations where what you need, in order to go on living, is to believe that you are a good person and destined for greatness. Although what you actually need to become a good person and to be destined for greatness is to confess to yourself that you are neither destined for greatness nor a very good person. The loop continues forever.

The Kotzker spoke: "You want to find the truth? Start by calling yourself a liar."

[40]

"What is this, a Zen monk?" wondered Jacob. (He may have lost his self-confidence, but at least he still had his brain.)

"You're a liar. You set up that whole scene with your mother overhearing your father asking Esau to fetch him some game. You arranged it so that she would tell another one of her secrets to her 'special little boy.' And you did it because you think you're the scion of the Jewish people."

Jacob could feel the sweat forming under his arms. This guy would not be easy.

"You have 'to scrutinize [your] motivations, purify [your] intentions, always be on guard against the intrusions of the ego. The first step to self-knowledge is self-doubt.'"

"In that case," Jacob fired back, "I've already taken the first several steps. Look at me: I sleep alone in the wilderness and don't know where I'm going."

"No, you still don't understand. You think that being unsure of yourself or feeling dejected is diminishing your ego, but you still are lying to yourself. In your heart of hearts, you hope this will only be a necessary setback on the way to even greater glory. Another disguise of arrogance. You see, 'The choice [is] between love of God and love of self ... and the only way to steer clear of the latter is to live in militant opposition to the ego.'"

As the sun rose, Jacob wondered how he had acquired such an enormous ego in the first place. Esau certainly didn't have one.

ROOM ENOUGH *for* ONLY ONE EGO

Kotzk deliberately misreads the verse in Deuteronomy in which Moses recalls his experience at Sinai and says, "I stood between God and you." Says Menachem Mendl, that

Self-knowledge is self-doubt
Heschel, *Passion for Truth*, 94.

Opposition to the ego
Ibid., 102.

Between God and you
Deuteronomy 5:5.

it is your I, "your ego that stands between you and God. Normally not even an iron barrier can separate Israel from God, but self-love, egotism will drive them apart."

Drive them apart
Mordecai HaKohen, *Al HaTorah* (Jerusalem, 1968), 489–90; *Itturay Torah*, 2:257, 6:43.

Room in this world
Talmud tractate *Sotah* 5a.

In other words, there is only room enough in this world for one ego, yours or God's. You pick. Paraphrasing the words of the Talmud, "The Holy One says of anyone who is conceited, there is only room in this world for one ego, yours or Mine."

How do you reconcile the mutually exclusive claims of your ego and God's? Feuerbach and Freud solved it by claiming that God's ego was a projection of our own. There was, they claimed, only our ego envisaged in the heavens. Eastern mysticism claims the opposite: Our individual human egos are illusory and all being exists within God's ego.

Classical patriarchal "king on a heavenly throne" religion claims that we must subjugate our ego to God's. We literally get down on our knees. Techniques for suppressing arrogance range from benign gestures of humility to life-denying forms of asceticism. But this has been a losing battle. Western religious history is a continuous string of failures to fashion a system capable of controlling the human ego without simultaneously mutilating the human being through guilt.

Idolatry believes there is a divine Ego that is accessible to human manipulation—not just cajoling, persuasion, or bargaining but actual control. Idolaters infiltrate heaven and remake God into their own images. They become their own gods. Jews tried it once at the very foot of Sinai.

EATING the GOLDEN CALF

The closest Jews come to an inherited corporate shame (akin to the Christian doctrine of original sin) is the *agel zahav*, the golden calf. A biblical paradigm of idolatry, the calf represents an act of depravity contaminating unborn generations. How instructive and ironic therefore that Moses made Aaron and the people grind up the gold and eat (that is incorporate) their own creation. The dust remains woven into the very tissue of our bodies as a bitter reminder of how easily ego imagines it can exploit God. And by consuming our own idol we are compelled to realize that not only is it our own creation, but that literally (to invert the Freudian dictum) what goes out also comes back in.

Grind up the gold
Exodus 32:20.

One can and must say, "Some of God is within me and some of me is in God." This is the root of all religiosity. To go beyond this and equate your ego with God is the root of all idolatry. And thus, any "thing" people worship in the hope of controlling God, with the intent of extending the power of their egos into the universe, is an idol.

The Torah is the instrument through which the prohibition against idolatry is preserved. Unfortunately, any attempt to manufacture a memento for an event like Sinai that defies physical representation runs the risk itself of becoming an idol. God has no body, but we remember this with the Torah, a tangible thing.

The WORDS on a TOMBSTONE

In Hasidism, the titles of books are frequently drawn from a biblical phrase that either contains or alludes to the author's own name. In this way title, author, and sacred text

[43]

are fused. Furthermore, since sacred text is ultimate reality, the title of the book takes on a spiritual dimension and becomes itself a pseudonym for the author. You are what you write.

> When the Baal Shem Tov was near his death, a student came to him with a hand-written book and said, "These are your words, which I have written down. This is the Torah of Rabbi Israel Baal Shem Tov." The Master read what was written and said, "Not one word of this is my Torah."

Not one word of this Meyer Levin, *Classic Hassidic Tales* (New York: Citadel Press, 1932), 163.

In Judaism, where "the word" is both the instrument of creation and the primary souvenir of God's love, books are sacred and writing flirts with idolatry. Every book by a human author is, after all, only a symbolic Torah; just as every writer hopes to supplant God by uttering a book good enough to be criticized and misinterpreted forever. Only God's Torah provides an infinite source of life and new meanings. The Baal Shem may have meant to refuse not authorship but a fixed text, wanting to keep his words (and himself) in motion as long as possible.

This perpetual fluidity also may be one of the few potentially religious dimensions of electronic word processing. As in the Torah, here too the letters themselves are only lights on the video monitor, moveable throughout the author's life. Only God's Torah, even though it is first encountered as "hard" ink on parchment, remains eternally fluid "soft" copy. The lights of its letters constantly rearrange themselves before our eyes, refusing to be still for even a moment.

The books of human writers can only continue to be incomplete until the day of the author's death. No more forthcoming editions with a new author's preface. The book is closed forever. What began as a modest literary attempt at self-deification thus becomes frozen into tombstone, a sepulchre carved deep into the rock. Like some Pharaonic tomb, religiously designed to remain unfinished until the last possible minute, the book now becomes a monument to our mortality, dead weight. Death means that our human Torahs can never be changed. We cover the walls of our lives with the hieroglyphs of our books and then spend eternity lying in the darkness reading and re-reading them, misspellings, typos and all. The Baal Shem Tov seems to have known better.

I'M GOD; YOU'RE NOT

Metaphors for Torah abound. Perhaps the most formatively potent is Torah as a total of 613 commandments, first postulated by Rabbi Simlai in the third century. Simlai, in all likelihood, never counted them. Instead he arrived at this number by adding together the number of days in the solar year (365) with the number of parts believed to be in the human body (248). There were, Simlai suggested, 365 prohibitions and 248 positive commandments. In this way the sum of the two numbers symbolically would encompass both the physical and the temporal universes. Several scholars have each taken turns at identifying precisely what was commanded. The most famous was certainly Moses Maimonides in the twelfth century. His enumeration of the "613," in *Sefer HaMitzvot* (The Book of the Commandments), became the primary source for subsequent Jewish legal tradition.

Rabbi Simlai Louis Jacobs, *A Tree of Life: Diversity, Flexibility, and Creativity in Jewish Law* (New York: Oxford University Press, 1984), 16.

Rabbi Hamnuna, a contemporary of Simlai, questioned why the numerical equivalent for the Hebrew word Torah is not 613 but only 611? According to the numerological system of *gematria*, each Hebrew letter is assigned a number value corresponding to its place in the sequence of the alphabet. Thus the four letters of the word *Torah, tav* (400), *vav* (6), *resh* (200), and *hay* (5), produce a number totaling 611. But this is two short of the total of Torah commandments according to Rabbi Simlai. If the discrepancy was fifty or even ten, there would be little concern, but to fall just two short demands an explanation. The solution permits Rabbi Hamnuna an insight that generates a modest category of research: which two?

Moses commanded us
Deuteronomy 33:4.

According to the Book of Deuteronomy, "Moses commanded us a Torah." Since "Torah" equals 611, we received 611 commandments from Moses. But the other two, we heard straight from God (*mi-pi ha-gevurah,* from the Mighty Mouth itself). And those two (according to the Jewish numbering of the commandments) are the first two utterances of the decalogue: "I am the Lord, your God...." and "You shall have no other gods before me...." These are the primary, unmediated religious content of Sinai; all the rest is human commentary.

Mighty Mouth itself
Talmud tractate *Makkot* 23b–24a.

Rest is human commentary
The idea of two utterances coming directly from God finds proof even in Psalm 62:11. "All the commandments in the Torah number 611, and two, which God spoke, as it is said, 'God spoke once, twice have I heard it.'" Midrash *Pirke deRabbi Eliezer,* ch. 41: Midrash *Mekilta DeRabbi Ishmael,* 2:228 n. 12.

These first two utterances are actually mirror images of one another. "I am the Lord your God...." and "You shall have no other gods before me...." We realize, after further scrutiny, that they also reduce themselves to: "I'm God; you're not." That is all you need to know to construct a religion. The Holy One of Being has an intention beyond your ken; it is other than you. God's ego is not yours. In the words of the prophet Isaiah, "My plans are not your plans." Not because you don't want to do what God wants, but because you can only comprehend a tiny part of God's plan. I'm God; you're not. This is the beginning of the reconciliation between God's ego and our own. This is also what Menachem Mendl of Kotzk may have taught Jacob: God can only be God when you are not.

Not your plans
Isaiah 55:8.

[46]

BREAK OFF YOUR EARRINGS

God is like truth or light, refusing to be contained within any static object. Once apprehended, truth ungratefully changes its beholder. For this reason, truth must be discovered again and again. Similarly, no sooner is the energy transferred to our optic nerves than the light ceases to be. For this reason, we do not see light; we consume it, again and again. The God, whose Name is Being, who has neither pronounceable Name, visible form, nor a voice that has any audible sound, is also literally unimaginable.

Supposedly Judaism's big idea is that there is one God. But many religions have this understanding, and most people figure it out on their own. Judaism's great unacknowledged insight is that God must not be represented in any physical form. I once led a discussion among children in the fourth grade about God. To begin, I asked them to tell me what they knew about God.

Not surprisingly, the first comment was, "God's invisible."
I then asked what God would look like if God were visible.
"God wouldn't look like anything," another answered. "Because God doesn't have a body."
"Maybe," ventured one very young theologian, "God is visible; it's just that there's nothing to see."

For this reason we not only should not, we cannot make an idol of God. Still, people try. Fetishes enable us to imagine we can sexually manipulate someone we love. In the same way, an idol permits the idolater to imagine God can be held in his or her hands. And, since neither a fetish nor idol has

Brought them to Aaron
Exodus 32:3.

Out came this calf
Exodus 32:24.

Less than idol-worship
Encyclopedia Judaica, s. v. "Kotzk."

any life of its own, it can be whatever we please. "And all the people took off the gold rings that were in their ears and brought them to Aaron." He explained it later to Moses, "I hurled [the gold] into the fire and out came this calf!" Just like that!

EGOTISM and IDOLATRY

It is taught in the name of Menachem Mendl: "The great hazard is that one will be filled with himself or herself, with conceit, with self-satisfaction, feelings which are nothing less than idol-worship...."

The first idol, and the one that makes us all idolaters, is not a statue, but the ego. I am not referring to that imaginary dimension of the psyche postulated by Freud, also called ego, but rather to a way of acting that says, "I judge us both, and I am more important than you."

Ego is not thinking you're a talented or a good person. That is only self-confidence, or, in extreme cases, ordinary conceit. Ego is arrogance. It is thinking that you are better than someone else. It is making yourself big in the presence, and at the expense, of someone else. A hermit cannot be arrogant. An ego needs someone else, another person, one you believe to be inferior to you, in front of whom you can preen, raise your chin, and stretch your beautiful neck.

The ultimate fantasy is not just judging yourself to be better than others but trying to make yourself so important that you imagine you can do whatever you please and still live forever. The entire Hebrew Bible can be understood as a chronicle of humanity's incessantly foiled attempts to do whatever they want, live forever, and thereby to be God. In this way both ego and idol attempt to displace God.

The prohibition against idolatry, in effect, also prohibits egotism, self-centeredness at the expense of someone else. Self-centeredness at the expense of someone else is the root of being a mean person. Therefore, the prohibition against worshiping idols is just a fancy theological way of saying, don't be self-centered. And the first two utterances at Sinai now mean: "If you let Me be God, then you won't be a louse," or conversely, "When you're a louse, there is no God!" The barrier between us and God is our ego, and the focus of the tension is the personal pronoun, I.

REDUNDANT PERSONAL PRONOUN

As in many languages, most Hebrew verbs contain their subjects. This obviates the need for personal pronouns to tell who is doing the acting. For stylistic reasons personal pronouns are occasionally used, but in the past and future tenses they are superfluous. Jacob's declaration, "Surely God was in this place and I, i did not know" is an example of such an unnecessary pronoun.

The verse literally reads, "Surely God was in this place and I, i did not know." The sense is "... and me, I didn't know." But the "I" (in Hebrew, *Anochi*, אנכי) seems to be redundant. Unless, of course, you assume, as Jews have done for millennia, that God does not waste words.

This simple "extra I" (which the school of Kotzk identifies as ego or conceit) leads Pinhas Horowitz, the author of a Hasidic commentary on the Torah, *Panim Yafot*, to an important insight. "It is only possible for a person to attain that high rung of being able to say, 'Surely God is in this place,' when he or she has utterly eradicated all trace of ego from his or her personality, from his or her sense of self, and from his or her being. The phrase, 'I, i did not know,' must mean, '*my* I—i did not know.'"

"The beginning of true piety is not so easy," whispered the Kotzker. "You must subdue your ego and call yourself a liar. It could make you lonely and a little crazy. A crazy man about God. You understand me?"

"Yes, I think so. God was here all along, and the reason I didn't know it is because I was too busy paying attention to myself."

Religious life demands constant vigilance against the schemes of our egos (the little *i*'s) to supplant the Divine.

LISHMA: *for the SAKE of ANOTHER SELF*

In Judaism, doing something entirely because of God's request, without any thought of personal pleasure or reward, is said to be *lishma*, for its own sake. Obviously to do something *lishma* is literally self-transcending. We have a beautiful example of this in a discussion surrounding the passage in Genesis where God says to Abraham, "Go forth from your native land.... And I will make of you a great nation, and I will bless you...." According to rabbinic tradition, this was the first of many subsequent trials that Abraham will have to endure.

Rabbi Aryeh Leib of Ger cites Rashi's comment that, according to the biblical text, leaving home was apparently for Abraham's own benefit. The Gerer goes on to ask how could this be a difficult test to endure if God promised Abraham great reward? Aryeh Leib answers his own question.

Actually this was an enormously difficult test for Abraham. For the biblical text says a few verses later that ultimately Abraham did not set out on the journey for his own reward but simply, "And Abraham went as God had told him." He went, in other words, *only because of the command of God*, without any other motive. The real test was whether, after all these assurances of reward, Abraham would be able to preserve the purity of simply doing as God wanted, without contaminating the act with his own motives or confusing it with his own benefit.

Enormously difficult test
Itturay Torah,
1:83–84.

The first test of the first Jew was not whether or not he would do what God said but whether or not he could do it *only* because God said it. Would he be able to put his self out of the way?

EGOLESSNESS in the SUKKA

During the Autumn festival of *Sukkot,* or literally "booths," God asks the Jewish people to dwell in temporary little huts. The roof is the key thing. It must be composed only of organic materials arranged densely enough to provide shade but not so dense as to obscure starlight. We spend a beautiful week contemplating the irrelevance of our other more permanent houses and our permanent relationship with the natural world. The weather does not always cooperate; sometimes it rains. And when it does, we are confronted with a religious decision: What constitutes enough rain to go inside. One ancient tradition says that it is permitted to go inside when the rain begins to dilute your soup!

Self out of the way
Rabbi Menachem Nahum of Chernobyl taught that "the point is rather to kill off selfhood, for 'Torah does not exist'—is not really alive and one with the source— 'except in the one who kills himself....' He has to kill his own self and act only for the goal of pleasing God."
Upright Practices, 186.

Still the pious are eager to continue beneath the *"sukka* of God's presence."

Rabbi Fishel of Strikov used to sit in the *sukkah* even during the rain. Once his students asked him, "Is it not written in the *Shulhan Arukh,* 'When it rains, a person should go inside,' and does not Rabbi Moses Isserles add in his commentary on this, 'Anyone who is exempt from dwelling in the *sukkah* and who does not leave it when it rains, receives no Divine reward and is simply a dummy'?" "Better I should be a dummy," replied Rabbi Fishel, and he remained alone in his *sukkah* in the rain.

Menachem Mendl of Kotzk says that it is all a matter of how important you think you are.

The concept of the *sukkah* is to totally annihilate the ego, completely nullifying the self before God. It is for this reason that one who is uncomfortable [with being a little wet] is exempt from the *sukkah.* When a person feels discomfort, this is an indication that he has not yet completely annihilated his ego, since if he had, he would not feel any annoyance whatsoever. Since he has not reached this level, he is exempt from the *sukkah.*

When it rains
Joseph Caro, *Shulhan Arukh,* vol. I, *Orah Hayim* (1565), par. 639.

Alone in his sukkah
B. Yeushson, *Meotzarenu HaYashan* (Jerusalem, 1978), 4:59.

Exempt from the sukkah
Aryeh Kaplan, *Chassidic Masters* (New York: Maznaim Publishing, 1984), 177; *Meotzarenu HaYashan,* 4:59.

HUMILITY

There is more to humility, however, than merely how you view yourself or your ego. Humility is a function of how you view others. Your attention is directed outward. Arrogance is making yourself great in the presence and at the expense of another; humility is realizing that, whatever your greatness, power, knowledge, grace, or even kindness, you are never greater than another.

Martin Buber teaches that humility, in classical Hasidism, is built around the notion that each person is unique and, therefore, precious. "In each person there is a priceless treasure that is in no other. Therefore, one shall honor each person for the hidden value that only this person and no one else has." Humility is not being in the presence of people who are better than we are, but simply being in the presence of people, any people, for they are all as unique as we are.

A priceless treasure
Martin Buber, *Hasidism and Modern Man,* trans. Maurice Friedman (New York: Harper & Row, 1985), 115.

Humility commences with the realization that no one is inferior or superior to anyone else. This fundamental egalitarianism then matures into a willingness to give of oneself to another. Until, finally, true humility generates a love for all creatures.

ACTS of SELFLESSNESS

In Judaism, the most elegant and commonly practiced method for subduing the ego is a loose catalog of acts called *gemilut hasidim,* usually translated as deeds of loving kindness. Acts of *gemilut hasidim* customarily include leaving unharvested produce in the corners of the field for the poor and the stranger, extending hospitality to wayfarers, visiting the sick, ransoming those held captive, providing clothing for the naked, feeding the hungry, dowering the impoverished bride, attending the dead to the grave, comforting mourners, showing deference to the aged.

Acts of selflessness
Talmud tractate *Shabbat* 127a; Mishnah tractate *Peah* 1.1.

Corners of the field
Leviticus 19:9–10, 23:22; Deuteronomy 24:19–21.

Hospitality to wayfarers
Genesis 18:3. Abraham tends guests.

Visiting the sick
Genesis 18:1. God appears to Abraham after his circumcision.

Clothing for the naked
Genesis 3:21. God makes clothes for Adam and Eve.

Attending the dead
Deuteronomy 34:6. God buries Moses.

Comforting mourners
Genesis 25:11. After Abraham's death God blesses Isaac.

Deference to the aged
Leviticus 19:32.

These deeds do not say, "You are more important," but "You are every bit as important as I am." In most cases repayment is unlikely. In one way or another, they all involve some form of selflessness in the service of someone else. They restrain the ego. In the words of Job, "I am dust and ashes." "Someone asked the Maggid [of Mezritch]... 'How do we achieve a state of ecstasy toward God?' And he answered him, 'He who requires fire, let him search among the ashes!'"

Dust and ashes Job 42:6.

Search among the ashes Joseph Weiss, "Via Passiva in Early Hasidism," in *Studies in Eastern European Jewish Mysticism*, ed. David Goldstein (New York: Oxford University Press, 1985), 85.

MAKING LOVE

Acts of loving kindness are more. Rabbi Ed Feld of Princeton University suggests that since the noun *hesed* means "grace," "kindness," or "love" and the verb *gamal* means "to recompense," "to do," or "to render," the idiom, *lig-mol hesed*, means "to cause love" and *gemilut hasidim* are actually "acts that cause love." Certainly they cause love in another; perhaps even more importantly, they awaken love in us.

The opposite of love is not hate but self-love. Indeed, the paradox of loving seems to be that you get bigger from making yourself smaller. Love cannot be acquired but only given. The love you give is the love you have. And the more people you love, the more love you have. Said one tsaddik, "How can you say of me that I am a leader of the generation when I still feel in myself a stronger love for those near me and for my seed than for all men?'"

Leader of the generation Ibid., 116.

Someone once asked Isaac Bashevis Singer which one of his books he liked the best. He responded with a question. "Do you have more than one child? If so, could you tell me which one you love the most?" The precious uniqueness of each creature makes them all equally beloved. You want to be like God? Start by trying to love all creatures with equal love! Get your self out of the way.

BUBER on the FINAL HERESY of KOTZK

In the introduction to the second volume of *Tales of the Hasidim*, Martin Buber suggests that Kotzk was the "final act" of the Hasidic drama.

> The crisis came on a Friday evening on which the rabbi did not pronounce the Benediction of Sanctification (*kiddush*) until midnight and did not leave his room to come to the Sabbath table until that time. The oral reports, almost all of which have been preserved, differ considerably on what happened then, but all agree on a certain more or less outspoken antinomian note, on the transference of Rabbi Mendl's inner rebelliousness to his relation to the Torah. This holds even though we do not know whether he really said the words attributed to him by the so-called enlightened group—that human beings with all their urges and lusts are part of God—and whether he finally cried out: "There is no judgment and there is no judge!"—or whether he only touched the candlestick and thus ostentatiously sinned against the law of the Sabbath....
>
> From that time throughout the remaining twenty years of his life, Rabbi Mendel kept to his room behind two doors that were almost always closed. Two holes were bored in one door through which he heard the daily services in the adjoining House of Prayer, presumably at times watching.

But sometimes, on a Friday evening, he issued from his room dressed in his white *pekeshe* and greeted his visitors, whom he otherwise gave only the tips of his fingers through the hole in the door.... When called to read the Torah on a Sabbath, he would go to the pulpit, his prayer shawl drawn over his face, and would go back again [to his room] as soon as he had read the scriptural portion.

Drawn over his face
Buber, *The Later Masters,* 42–43.

Other stories tell of how, towards the end, the Kotzker would appear on a small balcony, overlooking the prayer hall. He would survey the congregation and shout, "You're all liars!"

MY EGO, I DID NOT KNOW

"I have been lying to myself for a long time. Too long," mused Jacob. "I don't know if the secrets she tells me are because she loves me more than Esau or because she just thinks I need them and he doesn't." (This is where Jacob considers, for just a moment, that the world does not revolve around him.) The realization made him sad. Saying goodbye to an illusion or an old friend is sad. In this case the melancholy whispered the possibility of redemption. There might be other selves in the universe equally beloved by God and maybe even by Rebecca. And, at least for the time being, this discovery was unsettling but not devastating. If you can set your self aside, you will not perish. You will learn something about God.

אכן יש ה' במקום הזה ואנכי לא ידעתי

God is present, even in the midst of evil

3 / LUDOMIR

The OTHER SIDE

Hannah Rachel was the only child of Monesh Werbermacher of Ludomir, a town in the Ukraine. Her mother died when Hannah was yet a girl. A frail child, she spent a lonely and melancholy youth. Once, during a serious illness, she experienced a religious conversion. What makes her noteworthy and the reason she came to speak with Jacob is that she, a woman, became a famous *rebbe*, the *Ludomirer Maid*. Men came from miles around to learn from her. A synagogue was built with an adjoining apartment.

Hannah Rachel Werbermacher
Ludomir, Poland, 1805–1892.

[59]

And from there, during the third Sabbath meal, she spoke Torah to her Hasidim through a half-open door. Men learning from a woman they would not allow themselves to see.

Age of eighty-seven
Encyclopedia Judaica, s. v. "Maid of Ludomir."

Her popularity as a *tsaddeket*, a female *tsaddik*, or *rebbe*, effectively ended soon after her fortieth year, when she was persuaded to marry. Soon afterward she moved to Israel where she continued to conduct herself as a Polish *rebbe* and maintained a considerable following. In her later years she was involved in Kabbalistic attempts to bring the Messiah. She died at the age of eighty-seven in Jerusalem.

Scholars
S. A. Horodecky, *Ha-Hasidut ve-ha-Hasidim* (Tel Aviv, 1951), 4:68–71.

Scholars such as S. A. Horodecky and Ada Rapaport-Albert continue a lively debate over the amount of gender autonomy Hasidism allowed its teachers. Some see the Maid of Ludomir as an example of freedom, others as an "aberration of nature and a social deviation." Dr. Nehemia Polen reminds us of an old popular witticism that "a rabbi is made into a Grand Rabbi by the sign painter" and that the ability to attract people who seek blessing, counsel, and assistance remains the real test of any would-be *rebbe*. And by that standard, Hannah Rachel was a *rebbe*.

Aberration of nature
Ada Rapaport-Albert, "On Women in Hasidism, S. A. Horodecky and the Maid of Ludmir Tradition," in *Jewish History: Essays in Honor of Chimen Abramsky*, ed. Ada Rapaport-Albert and Steven J. Zipperstein (London, 1988), 495–525.

One mystery surrounds her career. Though everyone agrees that she was an extraordinary teacher, nothing she said has been preserved in writing or even in oral traditions. Was it because she was a woman? Or was it perhaps because she spoke from the other side of consciousness, "in the mother tongue," in metaphors incomprehensible to patriarchal language?

The sign painter
Nehemia Polen, "Miriam's Dance: Radical Egalitarianism in Hasidic Thought," in *Modern Judaism* 12, no. 1 (1992): 1–21.

Perhaps because her father was lonely he taught her everything he knew, things that women simply were not told, not supposed to know. His words fell like rain. Because she was a woman, she processed the teaching in new and beautiful ways and blossomed overnight into a lush garden of wisdom. Alas, unlike many of her gender, she was not very good at relating to others. They were only extensions of herself. She simply couldn't imagine that another person could be independent and discrete from her. Perhaps conversation for her was like speaking into a television camera, speaking through a half-open door to an unseen audience.

Jacob had listened to and learned from women before, but this one, instead of looking him in the eye as she spoke, addressed the distant mountains. She reminded him of his mother Rebecca whom this night he hated for making him the way he was and whom this night he loved for making him the way he was. He wondered what it would be like to be married to such a person.

"I never got to say good-bye to my mother," Hannah lamented. "I awoke one morning and ran to her bed, but she was already cold." As she spoke her eyes seemed to be searching the distance. "When you said God was here and you didn't know it, you were talking about yourself and what you had done. You were talking about finding God even in your most terrible urges. God is truly everywhere; yes, even in midst of evil."

ACTION in the EAST

Forget about a good person who contracts a terrible disease and dies prematurely or about a wicked one getting rich and living to a ripe old age. Let's go right to the core of the question about evil. Consider a random image from myriad nightmares and agonies human beings have inflicted on one another. It would inevitably come up sooner or later in the conversation anyway and, as it invariably does (and perhaps should), silence further discussion.

There is a wall-size photograph in *Yad VaShem*, Israel's memorial to those who perished in the Holocaust. Before us is a great empty field somewhere "in the East." Near the bottom, in the left corner, we see part of a huge (but, for this kind of "action," not atypical) mass grave. The ditch is large enough to contain perhaps a dozen suburban American houses. This freshly dug valley is already partially filled with the naked, bloodied bodies of men, women, young men, young women, little boys, little girls, children, infants. (Lime has been sprinkled on the bodies.) We know from other accounts that they are not all dead. Many in the ditch are merely wounded. We know further from written accounts of similar scenes that the mass of corpses and still-living bodies moves, bleeds, writhes, and moans. (It was strictly forbidden to take such a photo.)

In the center of the mural, at least as large as the viewer, there are three people: a mother, holding her infant child to her bosom, faces the trench. Just behind her, at point blank range, a young German soldier trains the sights of his rifle at the woman's head, about to shoot. (The end of the rifle barrel is no farther away from her head than the reader's eyes are from this printed page.) In the background there are clouds and the gently waving, autumn grass of this unnamed Polish field.

If there is a God, where was that God when this photograph was taken? God was there. See, we have a photograph. There is God, over there in the ditch, in the mother's terrified eyes, even in the psychosis of the Nazi soldier. There is God, an ashen reality, now almost two generations later, more mysterious and holy than ever. The question is not Where was God? but Why do human beings do such things? Blaming God not only absolves us but increases the likelihood that we will allow such horrors to happen again.

How could God allow such a thing? Why didn't God do anything? To ask such questions assumes that God occasionally intervenes in human affairs *without* human agency. Yet countless events remind us that God does not work like that. Indeed, while it contradicts literal readings of some sacred texts, we suspect that God never has. God did not die in the Holocaust, only the Deuteronomic idea of a God who, through suspending laws of nature, rewards and punishes people.

Biblical accounts of earth swallowing villains, seas splitting to save innocents, or wicked nations being blotted out seem now, in the aftermath of the Holocaust, clearly to be metaphors—never meant to be taken literally. If the world of the Bible were so ontologically different from our world today as to permit such divine intervention, then truths from such a time would be irrelevant. For us, the snowflakes and rays of sunlight fall without discrimination on righteous and wicked alike. This is simply how the world works. And all theology after the Holocaust must begin with this acknowledgment.

What then is left to talk about? What is evil and where does it come from.

BAD and EVIL

First of all many things are bad that are not evil. This is a very important but often overlooked distinction. "Bad" means "unfortunate," "painful," and even "horrible," but it does *not* mean that someone is necessarily responsible for what has happened. A freak accident, for which no one is to blame, for instance, is "bad," but it is not "evil." Other times "bad" means "unethical," "wicked," and "evil." We cry out that things should have been otherwise and that someone is to blame. And if the one who is to blame acted intentionally, then the "bad" is also "evil." So "bad" can mean either "unfortunate," as in "no one is to blame," or it can also mean "evil," as in "someone has caused this bad thing to happen."

This double meaning of "bad" probably reflects a time when human beings believed they were powerless in the face of whatever befell them and that everything that happened was caused by God. Indeed, to this day, we still blame God for all sorts of things that are simply "bad" and even for what are entirely human acts. And, of course, when we do, we absolve ourselves of responsibility.

God does not intervene in the affairs of people, at least not in the way a parent might step in to settle a fight between children, take one of them to a physician, judge between righteous and wicked, punish the guilty, reward the innocent. These things can and do occur, but only through human agency.

Therefore the question "Why is there evil in the world?" means "Why are human beings evil?" or "What is the origin of human cruelty?" Sometimes people suffer because of some evil they themselves or others did or did not do, and sometimes they suffer through no one's fault, although the range of accidents tends to diminish sharply with maturity and responsibility.

If we rule out "accidental" tragedies that could have been prevented had the victim not taken some voluntary risk, we are left with only freak, hopelessly unforeseeable accidents like a tornado or a rare illness. And if we hold our society similarly responsible, for example, for not creating adequate safety measures or directing its energy to the prevention of disease, then the list is diminished even further. How much misery might be prevented, for instance, if humanity chose to allocate its resources toward healing rather than war?

Whenever something bad happens and the guilty ones are too many, too powerful, too distant, or unknown, we blame God. After all, if God runs nature, large undefined parts of history, and anything else we cannot figure out, then the "bad" thing that happened must be the deliberate result of God's intention, an indirect result of God's powerlessness, or a consequence of God's inexcusable inattention. In other words, whenever we say that some terrible natural event was "bad" and mean it was "evil," then God must either be malevolent or punishing us. We have entered "cosmic-bogey-man theology." God has no escape.

TWO UNIVERSES

"Once you acknowledge that bad things happen and that people do evil things, there are only two options," said Hannah Rachel, "Satan and God." She took a handful of pebbles and dropped them in two small piles before him. "Alternate worlds. In every way except one, these worlds of strewn pebbles are identical. In both worlds the sun shines, people make love, children play and people do astonishingly terrible things.

"In one universe, people maintain their 'selves,' their sanity, and God by giving evil its independence. Such wickedness, they reason, could not possibly have anything to do with God. There must be some other non-God power that makes it real and gives it vitality, and with whom God is in eternal conflict. In such a universe, where the source of evil is other than God, sooner or later, one way or another, you wind up with some kind of demonic force, *sitra achra*, Other Side, devil, or Satan.

"In the second world, God is somehow part of the evil, present even in its depths. This is the meaning of our assertion that 'God is One.' A Oneness at the core of all being in whom everything—yes, even evil—ultimately converges. The source of all reality. If God is the source of all being and human evil is real, then God therefore must be in it also. The evil does not derive its being from some extra-Divine source. This is certainly what Job learns when God speaks to him from out of the whirlwind. God does not cause, tolerate, or even forebear the evil, but God, as with everything else in creation, is in it."

God is One
Deuteronomy
6:4.

**Out of the
whirlwind**
Job 38ff.

It's ALL GOD

And if God is everywhere, God is also in the perverse things we plan and even carry out. To be sure, God is less evident and less accessible than in acts of kindness, for example, but in them nevertheless. In the words of Rabbi Tsadok Hakohen, a student of the school of Mordecai Yosef of Ishbitz. "God is present even in our sins." And rejecting our sins only postpones the ultimate task of healing and self-unification. Such an acceptance of all of our selves is another way of finding God. Dr. David Blumenthal of Emory University offers a similar teaching.

Evil, in its most profound sense, is contingent upon God for its very existence. There would be no shells [or, shards] if there were no sparks.... God is everywhere, even in the impulse to rebel against God. Reality is one. At this point, evil ceases to be grasped as an independent seductive force; it collapses ontologically and falls by the wayside psychologically. One's consciousness is, rather, filled with God.

Filled with God David R. Blumenthal, *God at the Center: Meditations on Jewish Spirituality* (San Francisco: Harper & Row, 1987), 25.

Aryeh Kaplan, the contemporary philosopher, explains it thus:

The Baal Shem Tov taught that God is actually hidden within all evil and suffering, but that God only hides when people do not realize that God is there.... Ultimately, there is no barrier between God and people except that of our own making, and if one succeeds in removing this barrier, then all evil is revealed to be an illusion.

Revealed to be an illusion Aryeh Kaplan, *The Hasidic Masters and their Teachings* (New York: Maznaim Publishing, 1984), 21.

TALKING to the OCEAN

"Think of it this way," explained the Maid of Ludomir. "If the world is covered by an ocean, the ocean naturally would be implicated in everything that happened. But we would not blame the ocean for its currents, its waves, or its storms. The ocean simply is. In much the same way God's ubiquity does not mean that God is therefore in the business of causing, intending, or even tolerating human misery. Correcting those things is the business of human beings. That is why God made human beings in the first place."

"But can you talk to the ocean?" Jacob objected. "Can you have a personal relationship with it? Can you pray to it?"

"Of course you can. Anyone who has been near, in, or on the sea knows that it can be addressed. But it does not answer, at least not in words that could be played back on a tape recorder."

"Still I wish it could speak in words like my father or my mother used to speak."

But even if God did—and we have a tradition that God's voice at Sinai was the voice of each person's parents—it is not the audible words themselves we crave. The content, the inflection, the sound of the voice—they all pale in comparison to the loving presence of the Holy One.

HUMAN EVIL and TEARING APART

If the ocean is incapable of perpetrating evil, then why do people occasionally do horrible things? The obvious answer is because human free will, by definition, requires that we be free to choose between good and evil. But this only postpones the deeper problem: Why would anyone ever choose evil at all? Why would a human being ever do anything cruel? That is the question. According to Jewish legend, the pain of being a human being (and thus for many, the resultant evil that people do) originates in two primal, psycho-spiritual "tearings." Something is separated, rejected, and made "other." And the memory of the tearing, the wound, is just too painful to endure. (And indeed, when these "tearings," as they so often do, shape the parent-child relationship itself, the result, as the important work of Dr. Alice Miller demonstrates, is the psychopathology of child abuse. From parent to child, one generation after another. A contemporary definition of original sin.) And the social institutions and political states that people fashion naturally resemble their creators.

Psycho-pathology
Alice Miller, *For Your Own Good: Hidden Cruelty in Child-Rearing and the Roots of Violence* (New York: Farrar, Straus & Giroux, 1983).

[68]

In the first tearing, a part of ourselves is rejected and identified as "enemy." The second tearing involves every human being's traumatic separation from his or her parents, the process of individuation and becoming autonomous. Both are lifelong, unending struggles. In one we tear off a part of ourselves to maintain our own sense of goodness, and in the other we experience ourselves as having been torn away for our own good. They are both suggested by biblical and subsequent rabbinic legend. And important elements of each are expressed in Jacob's own life story. Esau, Jacob's twin brother, is made into an enemy. And Jacob must leave his parents, never to see them again.

AMALEK and ESAU

In order to understand the first tearing and the process that makes Esau an enemy, we must consider the legends surrounding Amalek, the paradigmatic enemy of the Jewish people. Emerging from the brief wilderness accounts of how, for no apparent reason, he fell upon the weary stragglers at the tail end of the Israelite wanderers, rabbinic tradition imagines that Amalek must be the progenitor of every subsequent enemy of the Jewish people. His very reason for living is to injure Jews. And, according to Deuteronomic injunction, Jews are commanded to blot out his memory for all time. (The commandment is specifically and paradoxically to remember to forget!) The ruthless Haman of the Esther story and the cruelty of Rome are mythically connected through the same malevolent seed: Amalek.

Remember to forget
Deuteronomy 25:17–19.

This is not the simple "good guy/bad guy" scenario it first appears to be. The rabbis go on to teach that the wicked Amalek is descended from a woman named Timna. And while Timna was once in love with Jacob, he wouldn't give

[69]

Jacob's nephew, Eliphaz
The Midrash identifies him with Job's comforter of the same name. Louis Ginzberg, *The Legends of the Jews* (Philadelphia: Jewish Publication Society, 1909), 1:421.

Eliphaz, Esau's son
Genesis 34:14.

Eliphaz's handmaid
Midrash *Genesis Rabba* 82.14.

Thinness of a membrane
Midrash *Pesikta deRab KaHannah* (*Shemini Atzeret*, 30); see also Lawrence Kushner, *Honey from the Rock: An Introduction to Jewish Mysticism*, 2nd ed. (Woodstock, VT: Jewish Lights Publishing, 2000), 40–41.

Ishmael
Born of Hagar. Genesis 16:15.

Midian
Born of Ketura. Genesis 25:2.

her the time of day. Thus spurned, she became instead a concubine of Jacob's nephew, Eliphaz. "And Timna was concubine to Eliphaz, Esau's son." She reasoned, "Since I am not worthy of being Jacob's wife, let me be at least Eliphaz's handmaid." Vindictively bitter over her rejection, she raised her family to hate Jacob and all his progeny, the children of Israel.

This messy family arrangement also means, of course, that Timna's father-in-law was Jacob's twin, Esau. And rabbinic tradition is quick to note that not only was Esau himself rejected, but that he once even shared a womb with Jacob. Nothing more than the thinness of a membrane separated Esau, the great-grandfather of Amalek, from Jacob!

Why did the Holy One create both the hell of *Gehenna* and the heaven of the Garden of Eden? In order that one may borrow room from the other. And how much space is there separating them? ... The rabbis said that they are right next to one another.... Not even the thinness of a membrane separated Esau and Jacob.

Jacob rejects Timna, Jacob rejects Esau. They would have loved to be, or once were part of him. Now they are "other." Now they are enemy. Being torn away, that is the source of the pain we feel and probably of the pain we, in turn, inflict on others. All humanity is a closed organic system. Pain put into the system sooner or later comes back to us. Generation after generation. What goes around, comes around.

In a similar vein, Dr. Joel Rosenberg of Tufts University has observed that perhaps it was no accident that the descendants of the rejected children of Abraham, Ishmael and Midian, were selected as the two Egypt-bound caravan drivers (the text confusingly first refers to them by one name and then by the other) who brought Joseph from out of the pit. These rejected children of the patriarch were the very instruments through whom Abraham's great-grandchildren would be carried down into slavery.

The UNNAMED WRESTLER

We now understand why the struggle between Jacob and Esau assumes such significance. That night, over two decades later, when Jacob is left alone on the other side of the Jabok, he wrestles with another being. Was it his conscience, an angel, the patron of Esau, a divine being, or perhaps a once-rejected side of himself? The text does say, "You have wrestled with beings divine and human...."

This possibility that the nocturnal battle involved God is born out in another constellation of legends. The Talmud imagines that the dust from their wrestling ascended all the way to the Throne of Glory itself.

Rabbi Joshua ben Levi explained it this way: Since the same word is used in both Genesis, "As he wrestled (*b'hay-avko*) with him" referring to the struggle, and in Nahum, "And the clouds are the dust (*avak*) of God's feet," alluding to the Throne of Glory, we may conclude that dust from their wrestling rose all the way to God.

Or, as Rabbi Aryeh Leib of Ger explains, since the form of Jacob is engraved on the Throne of Glory, then the effects of any earthly struggle with the Other Side also must affect the Throne on High. The battle is not between us and some independent power. The struggle goes on inside God. It is part

From out of the pit
Genesis 37:27–28.

Abraham's great-grand-children
Joseph is carried down into Egypt by both Ishmaelites and Midianites. Genesis 37:25, 28.

Beings divine and human
Genesis 32:29.

Dust from their wrestling
Talmud tractate *Hullin* 91a.

As he wrestled
Genesis 32:26.

Dust of God's feet
Nahum 1:3.

Affect the Throne
Itturay Torah, 2:304.

of God; it is part of ourselves. But the struggle is not against anything intrinsically evil. (Indeed, nothing is intrinsically evil.) This means that God somehow must be connected with Esau, the source of Amalek, the great-grandparent of all our enemies.

How else, for instance, can we explain the inclusion of chapter 36 of Genesis. Here is an entire chapter devoted exclusively to cataloging the progeny of Esau! But Esau is the enemy. Esau is Amalek and Rome. Why does the Hebrew Bible care for the names of the grandchildren of our enemies? Yet there, to our astonished indignation, they are listed. I have even heard one tradition that goes so far as to suggest this chapter may be the holiest in the entire Torah! (And we are left wondering if there is perhaps a corresponding genealogy of Jacob's children in the Torah of Esau.)

The unnamed night wrestler of Genesis 32 represents a dimension of ourselves that has been rejected and labeled as "evil other." It comes back to injure and name us during the night. And since it is still a part of ourselves we cannot bear to acknowledge, when we sense it in someone else, we are all the more frightened and angry. And often, failing to find it in someone else, we project it onto them anyway for this deludes and comforts us into feeling that we have utterly torn it away. Hating something in someone else is easier than self-reproach.

Once we realize that what we detest in another person only wants to be accepted, taken back, and loved, do we begin to diminish our own capacity for evil. By embracing what was never really other, we neutralize the evil. We heal and redeem it and, in so doing, we heal ourselves and God.

One final image may be helpful in understanding how what has been torn away can be redeemed. Early Hasidism developed a doctrine called "strange thoughts," or "lascivious thoughts during prayer." According to this teaching, one sure sign that we have attained a high level in prayer is that invariably we will be assailed by embarrassingly wicked thoughts. Our first inclination is to reject them at once, but, as everyone knows, this only gives them even greater power over our prayers. We must, counsels the Baal Shem, realize that such thoughts are in reality only rejected parts of ourselves that sense this time of great closeness to God and come out of our unconscious yearning for redemption. As Yaakov Yosef of Polnoye, a student of the Baal Shem Tov, used to teach his students:

> One must believe that "the whole world is filled with [God's] presence" and [as we learn from *Tikkunei Zohar*] that "there is no place empty of [God]." All human thoughts have within them the reality of God.... When a strange or evil thought arises in a person's mind while he is engaged in prayer, it is coming to that person to be repaired and elevated.

The whole world
Isaiah 6:3.

Repaired and elevated
Daniel C. Matt, "Hasidic Texts with Prefatory Note," *Studio Mystica* 10, no. 2 (Summer 1987): 7.

Hannah Rachel of Ludomir, whose eyes restlessly search the horizon for someone else, carefully explained to Jacob that he must learn how, as the Hasidim say it, to "find the root of love in evil so as to sweeten evil and turn it into love."

Turn it into love
Altmann, "God and the Self," 146.

The SETUP in the GARDEN

The second form of tearing that is responsible for human evil comes from parents and children separating from one another. The price a human being pays for growing into an autonomous adult is the pain of leaving home. I am now convinced the Eden story intuits this.

If God didn't want Adam and Eve to eat fruit from the tree in the center of the garden, then why put it right there, out in the middle of the garden where Adam and Eve could reach it? Why didn't God just hide the fruit somewhere deep in the forest? And then, equally puzzling, after putting the tree in the middle of the garden, why did God specifically tell Adam and Eve to be sure not to eat the fruit?

(Can you imagine telling an adolescent, as you leave the house, "You can do whatever you like, just don't ever go in the top drawer of my dresser." "Sure, Mom. Right, Dad. Thanks for the tip.") What a different world it would be if the forbidden fruit were on one unknown random tree hidden deep in some primordial garden. The chances are high that we might never have discovered it. We would all live in childhood eternal.

There is one rabbinic tradition that tells of God's creating other worlds and destroying them before our present universe. Each one was presumably deficient in some vital way. For all we know, God did try creating a world without the tree temptingly planted right in the middle of the garden. Or maybe there was a prior universe in which God neglected to forbid human beings to eat the fruit. Maybe God realized that Adam and Eve weren't clever enough on their own to figure out how to sin. After universes of infantile obedience, they remained tediously, predictably, and incorrigibly infantile.

"Yes, Daddy, yes, Mommy, whatever you want."
"This will never work," reasons God. "Better they should know some sin, estrangement, and guilt but at least become

autonomous human beings rather than remain these insipid, goody-two-shoes infants. But I can't just make them autonomous. If I did, their autonomy, their individuation, their independence would be a sham. They must earn it themselves. They must want it badly enough to pay a price. I'll let them make their own children, but first they must earn their autonomy."

I suspect it was for this reason, out of desperation, that God resorted to a "setup" that has come to be known as the expulsion from the garden of Eden. Eating the first fruit was not a sin but a necessary, prearranged passage toward human maturity. We have read it all wrong: God was not angry; God rejoiced at our disobedience and then wept with joy that we could feel our estrangement and want to return home.

The SNAKE WORKS for ME

I can just hear Adam and Eve now:

"You mean it was OK all along to eat the fruit?"
"I knew you would," says God. "Why do you think I put it right in the middle and then made such a big deal about not eating it. I made you. You think I didn't know what would happen. It was a setup. That forbidden fig has had your name on it since before I began the creation."
"What about the snake?"
"Sammy? Sammy, the snake! That snake has been working for me from day one! Sammy come out here and meet the folks...."

(Snake enters from offstage, removes his skin, revealing a handsome young man wearing a white suit. Takes a bow. The stunned crowd rises to its feet in applause.)

Chased out of the garden
One of my seventh-grade Bar Mitzvah students, Alex Hardy, opined that the expulsion was indeed the finishing touch to the creation of human beings.

"Then that means getting chased out of the garden wasn't a punishment?"

"Of course not. The day you left home, you became truly human. For on that day you had to begin working for a living and working to bring forth life. Trying to convince your progeny to do what you want and then realizing that if you succeeded, you would only produce mindless infantile extensions of yourself instead of autonomous men and women who could step forward in the noonday sun and call you a louse because you were behaving like one. You can make them do just what you want for the rest of their lives, or you can teach them everything you know and then hide in the corner with your hands over your eyes while they learn how to drive the damn thing. If I can do it with you, then you can do it with your children."

"But sometimes," whispered Adam and Eve, "we just miss you and want to be close to you, like when we would walk together in the Garden when we were little."

"I am truly sorry," said God, "but as every adult knows, no matter how graceful, every 'growing up' necessitates lifelong pain. And that hurt at the core of our soul is what renders normal people, on rare occasions, capable of great evil. People hurt others because they were hurt. And they were hurt because that is the price of adulthood. There is no other way."

I once met a man in his mid-fifties. He seemed to me to be a kind, gentle man with the face of a child. He had never married. The other members of his family explained that the reason he had such an innocent face was because he had lived physically and emotionally with his mother for his entire life. I met him for the first time at the funeral of his mother. If he had committed any sins, he was as innocent of them as a child. And, at least until her death, all his pain could be soothed by his mother's love. For him the ultimate separation was delayed so long that, alas, it was probably too late for him ever to become an adult. So, you see, the choice is not whether or not to separate from your parents but only when.

What Adam and Eve did in the garden of Eden was not a sin; it is what was supposed to happen. Indeed, it has happened in every generation since. Children disobey their parents and, in so doing, complete their own creation. Adam and Eve are duped, not by the snake, but by God. They were lovingly tricked into committing the primal act of disobedience that alone could ensure their separation from God, their individuation, and their expulsion from (childhood's) garden. Yet just because such is the way of the world does not mean there is no psychic damage.

The price of autonomy, individuation, is the trauma of separation from parents. At the core of every psyche lies a deep pain. We are not guilty *because* of Adam and Eve's sin, as in orthodox Christianity's doctrine of original sin. Nor are we sinful *as* Adam and Eve were sinful, as in Judaism's teaching. For our own good we have been tricked into leaving our parents' home, into separating from God. The issue is not sin, guilt, or even disobedience. The necessary price for becoming an autonomous adult is the unending pain of separation.

Jacob wondered now if perhaps his mother had engineered the whole thing, maybe in order to fulfill that prophecy before he was born, or maybe just to get him out of the

Prophecy before he was born Genesis 25:23.

[77]

Really Esau or not
Genesis 27:18, 20, 21, 22, 24.

Flee at once to Haran
Genesis 27:43.

house. He thought about how his father had kept asking him over and over again if he were really Esau. Maybe he was in on it from the beginning too. And Jacob remembered the last words Rebecca had spoken to him, "Now, my son, listen to me. Flee at once to Haran...."

FULL of LIGHT

The Midrash offers the following parable in the name of Rabbi Isaac:

A castle in flames
Midrash *Genesis Rabba* 39:1; Abraham Heschel, *God in Search of Man* (New York: Farrar, Straus & Giroux, 1955), 113, 367.

> Once there was a person who was traveling from place to place and saw a castle in flames. "Could it be," wondered the traveler, "that this castle has no caretaker?" Whereupon the owner [suddenly] appeared and said, "I am the owner of this place." So it was with Abraham, our father, who [when he saw the evil in the world] said, "Could it be that the world has no owner?" Whereupon the Holy One of Being appeared and said, "I am the God of the Universe."

The castle could either represent the world or the self, and the Hebrew, *doleket,* in addition to meaning "in flames," can also be read "full of light." Now the parable reads: Once there was a person who was traveling from place to place and realized his soul was in flames and set for destruction. "Could it be that my soul has no caretaker?" Whereupon the Owner appeared and said, "I am the owner of this place." And so his soul was now filled with light.

God is present, though not immediately apparent, within the palace of the world and the world of the soul. First in the flames, the pain that continually assaults any sensitive human being, and then—once we realize God's presence—despair and wickedness give way to light, healing, and even joy.

GOD HAS BEEN HERE ALL ALONG

Jacob was awake just before dawn. He lay wrapped in a blanket, feeling the dew on his face. He thought about what he had dreamed and what he had exclaimed. And he remembered Hannah Rachel's explanation: "When you said that God was in this place and you didn't know, you realized that God had been involved from the beginning."

Jacob wondered now if God hadn't been a player all along. Perhaps that was the real meaning of the dream: not so much that the deal between himself and God was still on, not even that God would bring him safely back to this place, but that God had been present throughout the whole fiasco. Since before he was born. The prophecy about the older serving the younger, the birthright and the lentil stew, his father's "taste for game," his jealousy of Esau, his mother's conniving, his dressing up in a fur coat, stealing the blessing, everything.

Thinking this way about what he had done still made him feel ashamed but not devastated. He could at least imagine trying, as Hasidism would say, "to raise and sweeten" the evil devisings of his heart. To let them be a part of God's plan without hurting others at the same time. He could imagine trying to take the pain he now realized was deep inside him and instead of hurting others to simply cry instead. He could even imagine how, perhaps in some safe, future place, he might again someday be able to discern God's presence and the outline of some kind of plan. But he also knew, deep in

Healing, and even joy Altmann, "God and the Self," 146, cites Rabbi Nachman of Bratslav who interprets our verse, "Surely, God is in this place, and I, i did not know," as meaning that God can be found even in the midst of evil.

his gut, that most of the time such retrospective consolation would be concealed from him.

SWEETENING the EVIL in YOURSELF

We go down into ourselves with a flashlight, looking for the evil we have intended or done—not to excise it as some alien growth, but rather to discover the holy spark within it. We begin not by rejecting the evil but by acknowledging it as something we meant to do. This is the only way we can truly raise and redeem it.

We lose our temper because we want things to be better right away. We gaze with lustful eyes because we have forgotten how to love the ones we want to love. We hoard material possessions because we imagine they will help us live more fully. We turn a deaf ear, for we fear the pain of listening would kill us. We waste time, because we are not sure how to enter a living relationship. We even tolerate a society that murders, because we are convinced it is the best way to save more life. At the bottom of such behavior is something that was once holy. And during times of holiness, communion, and light our personal and collective perversions creep out of the cellar, begging to be healed, freed, and redeemed.

Rabbi Yaakov Yosef of Polnoye taught:

Turn aside from evil
Psalm 34:15.

Turn the evil into good
Matt, "Hasidic Texts," 7.

The essence of the finest *teshuva* [the returning to one's Source in Heaven] is that "deliberate sins are transformed into merits," for one turns evil into good, as I heard from my teacher [the Baal Shem Tov], who interpreted the "Turn aside from evil and do good" to mean: "Turn the evil into good."

[80]

(When Hannah Rachel Werbermacher finished her morning prayers, she would look at her left hand, wrapped in the bands of her *tefillin*. It was a black leather cube, two inches square, containing four passages from the Torah and held in position just above her biceps by a black leather strap. This in turn was spiraled around her forearm and wrist, and then plaited around the palm of her hand and between her fingers so that it spelled the Name of God. According to tradition, this act of loving service was reserved for men. Women were forbidden to wear the boxes. Yet there before her eyes was her defiant hand, swaddled, bridled, and subdued by the black leather straps. Now her left side and all its defiance was ready to re-direct its energy in holy ways. Now this "other side" was no longer her foil but a mighty companion. Sometimes she would even inconspicuously kiss it before removing the square, black box.)

Black leather cube Deuteronomy 6:8.

The conclusion of true *teshuva*, returning to our Source in Heaven, is not self-rejection or remorse, but the healing that comes from telling ourselves the truth about our real intentions and, finally, self-acceptance. This does not mean that we are now proud of who we were or what we did, but it does mean that we have taken what we did back into ourselves, acknowledged it as part of ourselves. We have found its original motive, realized how it became disfigured, perhaps beyond recognition, made real apologies, done our best to repair the injury, but we no longer try to reject who we have been and therefore who we are, for even that is an expression of the Holy One of Being.

We do not simply repudiate the evil we have done and sincerely mean never to do again; that is easy (we do it all the time). We receive whatever evils we have intended and done back into ourselves as our own deliberate creations. We cherish them as long-banished children finally taken home again. And thereby transform them and ourselves. When we say the *vidui*, the confession, we don't hit ourselves; we hold ourselves.

The Maid of Ludomir looked at Jacob. He did not look like a man who was having an epiphany. (Meeting your other side may be a sacred experience but it is also terrifying.) Dismay was all over his face. She didn't want to talk theology, she just wanted to hold him, to soothe this frightened wanderer. "Jacob, *Yaakov*," she whispered.

"That's me," he replied, "Jacob, *Yaakov*, the one whose name in Hebrew means 'heel.'"

"You are neither good nor bad; you are simply a human being. I know what I am about to say will be hard for you to understand, but it has been truly an honor to talk with you."

The TRUTH of a NAME

"And [Isaac] asked, 'Which of my sons are you?' And Jacob answered his father, 'I am Esau....'"

I am Esau
Genesis
27:18–19.

"Asked the [unnamed night wrestler], 'What is your name?' And [Jacob] replied, 'Jacob.' Whereupon the nameless one responded, 'Your name shall no longer be Jacob, but Israel....'"

Jacob,
but Israel
Genesis
32:28–29.

Jacob tells
the truth
I am grateful to
Judith Himber
for this beautiful insight.

This time Jacob tells the truth! Now, over two decades later, he manages to unify both sides of his personality. And the minute he tells the truth about his identity to the nameless-night wrestler, his other side, his twin brother, (God?), he is transformed into Israel. Now he is a being who has struggled with beings human and divine and survived. He rises to his destiny.

אכן יש ה' במקום הזה ואנכי לא ידעתי

*God was here because I stopped being
aware of myself*

4 / MEZRITCH

SELF-REFLECTION

Dov Baer once said to his disciples, "I shall teach you the best way to say Torah, to offer your innermost teaching. You must cease to be aware of yourself. You must be nothing but an ear which hears what the universe of the word is constantly saying within you. The moment you start hearing what you yourself are saying, you must stop." Ultimate self-expression and creativity is a primary process that precedes not

Dov Baer of Mezritch
Mezritch, Poland, d. 1772.

Cease to be aware
Buber, *The Early Masters*, 107. "Not to be aware of oneself but as an ear harkening to the way in which the 'World of Speech' speaks within you. It is not yourself who speaks. As soon as you hear your own words, stop." Weiss, "Via Passiva," 79.

only evaluation and censorship but even the very knowledge that one is speaking.

The *Maggid* (or storyteller) of Mezritch, as Dov Baer is also known, was one of the Baal Shem Tov's four disciples. After the master's death, leadership of the new Hasidic movement fell to Dov Baer, and in the Polish town of Mezritch Hasidism was transformed from a collection of spiritual insights into a religious movement. For Dov Baer the primary goal of a religious life was *devekut*, or cleaving to God. *Devekut* means that through her every act a person knows that she is an instrument of God's intention. Even in Dov Baer's later years, when he was afflicted with a disease that confined him to bed, he continued to teach ways of remaining continually in God's presence.

THREE SELVES

"In order to be aware of yourself," explained the *Maggid*, "a part of you must be looking at the rest of you. You have deliberately broken off a piece of your consciousness, set it a few inches over your shoulder, and you depend on this little piece of knowing to inform the remainder of your consciousness that it is you."

"Is that bad?" asked Jacob.

"No, in fact it is necessary for most things people do. Sooner or later each task requires that you become aware that you are the actor. 'Do I like the job I have done?' 'How do I appear to others?' 'Which is the best way to improve myself?' Again and again, you must remind yourself that you are you."

"But you just said the goal was to forget your self."

"Yes, that is the ultimate goal. But you must understand that there are three stages of self." The *Maggid* described some ordinary people who were hard at work. "The first stage is simply earning a living. Preoccupied with mouths to feed, needing sleep, and, if they are lucky, finding some leisure to sit down and rest, they do not have time to ponder whether or not they have selves or the designs of the Holy One of Being. For them it is enough to attend the house of prayer in the morning and the evening, give a little to charity, observe the Sabbath.

("My father, Isaac, once carried wood," mused Jacob to himself.)

"Then there are the ones who are driven to ask questions." Now Dov Baer asked Jacob to envision a room filled with life-long students scattered about the hall in quiet study, whispered conversation, rhythmic prayer, or restless sleep. "These are the ones who know that they have selves. Afflicted with the ancient questions of who they are and who God is, they sit with their feet in cold water so they can stay awake a few more hours and read just another page or two of Talmud, driven by the hope that the answer will be on the next page, condemned by self-reflection to be aware they themselves are the ones who are searching."

"Some, the third kind," he glanced at the first beams of sunlight now turning the night sky into dawn, "are no longer aware of their selves. They are very close to God."

"Then what is the difference between them and the first group of people who were preoccupied with earning their living?" asked Jacob.

"Not much. Maybe only that they have gone on the journey and returned to precisely the same place from which they began," shrugged the master.

MY DINNER with BUNAM

Rabbi Hanokh told of how, for a year, he yearned to go to his *rebbe*, Simha Bunam, and talk. But whenever he came in his master's presence, he was overcome with embarrassment. Finally it happened that one day he was hiding in the field behind Bunam's home, confused, terrified, weeping. Bunam noticed him off in the distance, went to the door, and motioned to him to come inside. "Why are you crying, Hanokh?" asked the *rebbe*. Whereupon Hanokh blurted out, "I am alive; I have arms and legs, eyes and ears; but I do not know why I have been created!" "Dummy," replied Bunam, "I don't know why I have been created either. C'mon, let's have dinner together!"

Dinner together
Buber, *The Later Masters*, 251.

WASHING the DISHES

The great insight of religion is not that we can find God in everyday life; it is that finding God returns us to everyday life. Forgetting one's self, making the self as nothing, gives us life beyond thinking and theology, beyond the incessant self-reflecting that renders us voyeurs of our own lives.

I once attended a *Brit Mila*, a ritual circumcision, at which the father was so preoccupied with photographing the event for posterity that he managed to avoid realizing what was taking place until it was over. (He had his reasons, though most of the time there are none.) We are so preoccupied with watching, recording, and analyzing our lives that we fail to live them.

We are afflicted with a compulsive need to put all creation into words, arrange them in one long string of sentences, and resolve every logical contradiction and inconsistency.

[88]

Allowing one's self to be nothing means that when we are done with our sophisticated-sounding sentences, the dishes must be washed. Beyond nothing-to-think is life-to-be-lived.

The story is told that a disciple of Shmelke of Nikolsburg asked his *rebbe* to teach him the mystery of serving God. The *tsaddik* told him to go to Rabbi Abraham Hayyim, who in those days was still an innkeeper. The student did as he was instructed and took up residence in the inn for several weeks. During all this time he failed to observe any special indication of holiness in the man. He seemed only to attend to his business. Finally, in desperation, the disciple went up to the innkeeper and asked what he did all day.

"My most important job," said Rabbi Abraham, "is to make sure the dishes are cleaned properly. I do my best to make sure that no trace of food remains on the dishes. I also clean and dry the pots and pans carefully so that they do not rust."

"That's it?" asked the student incredulously.

"That's it," replied the innkeeper.

Whereupon the disciple returned home and reported what he had seen and heard to his master.

"Now you know everything you need to know," Rabbi Shmelke said.

Now you know everything Buber, *The Early Masters*, 191–92.

RITUALS of the MIND

So why have religion at ail? Why not just live and enjoy life? Because sooner or later we all lose that childlike ability to simply live each moment without reflection. We ask ourselves the great question. Overwhelmed by the mystery of existence, we are embarrassed to hear ourselves whisper,

"Who?" The question comes in many disguises and according to many timetables. For some, it takes shape only over decades. For others, the world is shattered in an instant. But sooner or later the question comes to every human being.

Now since the question is also a question about the one who is asking the question, it cannot be answered by ordinary answers. Rational, "head" answers will not do. Like the question, the answer must involve the one who asks. And this requires some device like a walk in the forest, intense concentration, a slap in the face, or, of course, most effectively, the performance of religious ritual. It could be dietary, charitable, liturgical. They all set life in a new perspective. Nothing physically changes; everything remains just as it has been. Sleeping, washing, eating, doing the dishes, even asking ultimate questions—only now these things are done from a new vantage point, in a different mode.

Ritual, we realize, asks us to do very simple things with childlike devotion. But we soon realize that once we have performed them enough times to "master their moves" and shed our self-consciousness, our mind wanders. To our embarrassment, we realize we cannot do even simple religious acts without thinking about other things. (Our love life is contaminated by fantasies of loving someone else.) And rituals are requests by God, that is, the One who is at least the source of our selfhood, our very individuality. The ground of my being asks that I ritually recite six words proclaiming God's unity each morning, and I can't even keep my mind from wandering!

Religious rituals are a funny sequence of things we do to help us remember that we have forgotten why we have been created, and gently provide us with the instruments of return. They are ancient techniques for sending us back to everyday life with a childlike sense of wonder.

RACQUETBALL

This is also the germ of an old trick for how to win at racquetball or, for that matter, any sport where victory demands holding an object with total concentration. As you enter the court (or the green or the batter's box), ask your opponent how he holds his thumb on the racquet. His attention will be diverted from the game and onto his thumb, his consciousness split; his body will be there trying to play the game, but a part of his head will be somewhere else, looking at his thumb on the racquet.

SPEAKER of the SELF

You ever talk to yourself? I don't mean when you were alone in the car. I mean did you ever ask yourself a question to find out if you knew the answer? Like, "Who am I?" or "What is the meaning of my life?" Did you ever get an answer? What would you do if the answer were: "Who wants to know?" In other words, when you talk to yourself, who's talking and who's listening?

One of the discontents of civilization is the split between who we are and who is speaking. We are afflicted with a linguistic schizophrenia, disjunctive personalities. Call it the reflexive self: some other person living in there. A piece of consciousness broken off from awareness. And the fact that we can hold these interior conversations with our "selves" means that we are fragmented, alienated, broken. If we were

[91]

whole, then there could be no conversation, because there would be no one else "in there" to talk to.

Such self-reflecting mind games are the enemy of religious experience. In cinema, my son tells me, this is called "breaking the fourth wall," or alienation effect. The actor suddenly turns to the camera and speaks to it as if to a real person, jarring the viewers into realizing they are only watching a movie. The spell is broken.

The DANCER and the DANCE

Too much concentration can be worse than none at all. I remember how once in the presence of my teachers, I tried so hard to sing the *kiddush* (the prayer over the wine sanctifying the Sabbath) properly that I lost the melody and then even the words. The goal seems to be how to do something with all your heart without forgetting the sanctity of what you're doing.

There is a story about how Rabbi Hayyim of Krosno, another disciple of the Baal Shem Tov, once stopped with his students to watch a man dance on a rope strung high between two buildings. Rabbi Hayyim became so absorbed in the spectacle that his followers asked him what he found so fascinating in such a frivolous circus performance. "This man," he explained, "is risking his life, and I am not sure why. I am sure that while he is walking on the rope, he cannot be thinking that he is earning a hundred gulden; he cannot be thinking about the step he has just taken or the step he is going to take next; he cannot even be thinking about where he is; if he did, he would fall to his death. He must be utterly unaware of himself!"

Utterly
unaware of
himself
Ibid., 174.

[92]

Similarly, my teenage daughter once explained to me, "You cannot dance if you are worried about what you look like on the dance floor. You must give yourself to the music; let it tell you what to do; quit being so self-conscious. The only way you will ever know you are dancing is if, once the music has stopped, you didn't realize you were dancing."

In our congregation we have a dance on *Simchat Torah*, the celebration when we complete the annual reading of the Torah and commence anew. Many years ago, my wife came up with the idea that we unroll the entire scroll, and the members of the congregation, each holding a section, form one huge circle. It is a thrilling sight. After symbolically reviewing the entire five books of Moses, the Torah is then rerolled and the Klezmer Conservatory (Yiddish Revival Jazz) Band begins to play. People come from far and wide. The dancing goes on for hours.

I once asked a newly-arrived Soviet Jewish refusenik what he thought of our *Simchat Torah* celebration. To my surprise, he told me that while it was very beautiful, in Leningrad *Simchat Torah* was better. (In Leningrad *Simchat Torah* is the one occasion each year when the entire refusenik community gathers in front of the synagogue. They are rightly suspicious of what and whom the Soviet government allows inside). I was curious and a little insulted by his response. "How is it better?" I asked.

"In Leningrad," he explained, "if you dance in front of the synagogue on *Simchat Torah*, you must assume that the secret police will photograph everyone. This means that you will be identified and sooner or later your employer will be notified. And since such a dance is considered anti-Soviet, you must be prepared to lose your job! So you see," he went on, "to dance on such an occasion, this is a different kind of dance."

I wondered whether I would have the spiritual courage to give myself so completely to any dance. Or, for that matter, what it would be like to do anything with one's whole being? To let one's self be as nothing.

In the LIKENESS

When we manage to be nothing, even for a moment, we paradoxically make ourselves into the likeness of God who, after all, has precisely no likeness whatsoever. Genesis' saying that we are made in the likeness of God does not mean that God looks a little like us, with a face and a body, arms and legs, but that at the time of the creation of the first man and woman, human beings did not know or care about a tangible likeness, about the fact that they had bodies. The awareness of them is an invention of the human self, idolatrously preoccupied with wanting something to look at in the mirror. Once we managed to split our primal un-self-awareness into a self that is able to see itself as residing in a body, we conclude that God too must be embodied. And what better a body than a human body? To paraphrase Spinoza, if a pencil could look at itself in the mirror, then God would look like a pencil. The trick is to leave our self awareness or, as Dov Baer said, to empty ourselves, regard ourselves as nothing. Again and again in Jewish tradition, the fleeting dream of emptiness reappears.

In the words of Rabbi Yehiel Mikhal of Zlotchov:

It is the opposite of what people imagine: When they are not attached to the Creator but to earthly things, they think that they themselves exist [*yesh*] and are important and great in their own eyes. [Yet how] … can they be great when one night they exist and the next they are lost? Their days are as passing shadows, and even in their lives they are vanity. Thus if they think that they exist, then they certainly do not. This is not so if they think that they are nought because of their attachment to the Creator.

Consequently, they who cleave with all their mental powers to God … [they have lost their] existence like a drop which has fallen into the great sea and has come to its root and therefore is one with the waters of the sea and it is not possible to recognize it as a separate thing at all.

Like a drop
Weiss, "Via Passiva," 88–89.

FACE to FACE

This frustrated desire to "see" God constitutes the hallmark of Moses' humanity. If Moses were in any way divine, he would be limitless and bodiless. He would not need to ask permission to see God. But he is human. At the burning bush he is afraid to look, and by the time of the giving of the Torah at Sinai it is too late.

Moses was tending the flock.... The Lord appeared to him in a fire's flame inside a bush.... When the Lord saw that he had turned aside to look, and God called to him from within the bush.... And He said, "I [*Anochi*, אנכי] am the God of your father, the God of Abraham, the God of Isaac and the God of Jacob." But Moses hid his face, for he was afraid to look at God.

Afraid to look at God
Exodus 3:1–6.

[95]

Years later,
at Horeb
Exodus 33:18.

Don't want
to see you
Exodus 33:20.

Moses
hid his face
Midrash
Exodus Rabba
3.1, 45.4.

Years later, at Horeb, Moses begs to see God, but now God is no longer in the mood. "A person may not see Me and live," "Now I don't want to see you!" Rabbi Joshua ben Korcha said, "Too bad that Moses hid his face [at the bush], for had he not withdrawn, God would have revealed to him what was above and what was below, what had been and what was yet to be!"

Alas, only in the retrospect of an entire lifetime can the wish be granted to Moses, or any of us. We read in the closing verses of the Torah, after he is dead and buried, that "Never before in Israel has there been a prophet like Moses, who knew God *face to face*."

Knew God
face to face
Exodus 34:10.

We cannot see our own faces without a mirror, and even then the image is reversed. And we cannot know the presence of God until God has departed. If we knew that God was there, while the encounter itself was happening, more than the spell would be broken. In order to be present in God's presence, all our awareness must be there. Especially and including that part of consciousness that normally tells the rest of consciousness that we are present. But, of course, this means that some of our awareness is not there. As psychiatrist Arthur Deikman notes, "We *are* awareness, and that is why we cannot observe it; we cannot detach ourselves from it because it is the core experience of self."

We *are*
awareness
Arthur J.
Deikman, *The
Observing Self:
Mysticism and
Psychotherapy*
(Boston:
Beacon Press,
1982), 103.

See *achorai*,
my back
Exodus 33:23.

When God says to Moses at Horeb, "I will let you see *achorai*, my back," the Hebrew is not, as frequently misunderstood, anthropomorphic. The word *achorai* also has a temporal sense. What God says means, "Moses, you cannot know Me at the time when I am present. That would only mean that some part of your brain was hiding behind a rock trying to observe what was going on. No, Moses, you can only see *achorai*—what it's like just after I have been there."

Only then does Moses understand. Now he is able to lead the children of Israel through the wilderness. Now he remembers the first time he met God and was afraid to look. Now he realizes that the bush was a metaphor for his self. Now he sees that a person can be fully present, lose all awareness of self, and yet miraculously not be consumed by the "flame" of God's presence.

An EMPTY THRONE

The chair of Rabbi Nachman of Bratslav is empty. His Hasidim decided that no one could fill it and never appointed a successor. After his death, the chair was smuggled out of the Ukraine board by board and now sits on the second floor of the Bratslaver Synagogue in the *Mea Shearim* quarter of Jerusalem, on a small platform just to the right of the reader's desk. I was astonished as I prayed there several years ago to find how easily the presence of a *rebbe* who had been dead for two centuries could be evoked. I was reminded that being empty is not always the same as not being there.

Fittingly then Rabbi Nachman's last tale "The Seven Beggars" contains one of the great fantasies of nothingness in Jewish literature. The scene is a memory competition, rich with Eden's imagery. The contestants vie to see who has the earliest memory. One remembers "when they cut the apple from the branch." Another, remembers "when the fruit first began to be formed." Still another remembers "the taste before it entered the fruit." Finally, the blind beggar, who is telling all this, says, "I ... was yet a child, but I was there

Chair of Rabbi Nachman In recent years it has been refurbished and entirely enclosed in a glass museum case. Commenting on Genesis 28:16, Nachman of Bratslav says, "The goal of knowing is [to get to a point where one] doesn't know ... to nullify one's self and realize that one knows nothing at all." *Torat Natan* (Bnei Barak, Israel), 150.

[97]

too.... I remember all these events. (*Ikh gedenk gornicht*) I also remember nothing." And they answered: "This is indeed an older memory than all."

I also remember nothing
Arthur Green, *Tormented Master: A Life of Rabbi Nahman of Bratslav* (Tuscaloosa: University of Alabama Press, 1979), 344–45.

At every ritual circumcision there is an empty chair. The legend goes that the prophet Elijah was angry with Israel. He became convinced the Jewish people had irreparably severed the covenant. Therefore God decreed, as a loving punishment, that Elijah must be present at every future re-enactment of the covenant. In this way, except for a few moments when the infant is placed on Elijah's chair, the *kesay shel Eliyahu*, remains empty.

The most important empty chair, of course, was in the Solomonic temple. Johannes Pedersen, the Danish Bible scholar, explains the architecture of the holy of holies.

> From Ezekiel's description we may, then, infer that ... before the destruction of the temple, there was in its inner sanctuary a throne, the base of which was supported by cherubic beings. These again rested on wheels.... [This] seems to indicate that the throne was wheeled out in processions, perhaps within the precincts of the sanctuary. In all probability the throne was empty; Yahweh's honor might dwell there without any visible image.

The throne was empty
Johs. Pedersen. *Israel: Its Life and Culture,* 2nd ed. (London: Oxford University Press, 1940), vols. 3–4, 248.

The holy of holies was so sacred that, according to Rabbinic tradition, only the High Priest could enter, and even he could only do so on Yom Kippur (next to the Sabbath, the holiest day of the year). If, God forbid, he should drop dead of a heart attack while inside, no one could go in even to retrieve his corpse. So they tied a rope around his leg.

Once inside the holy of holies, he had to do only one thing. And he had prepared to do this for months. He would utter the *Shaym HaMeforash*, the ineffable four-letter Name of God. *Yod, Hey, Vav, Hey.* It is a name made from the three letters of the Hebrew alphabet that function primarily as vowels. How do you pronounce all the vowel sounds at once? The reason that God's Name is unpronounceable is because the Name of Being is the sound of breathing. The High Priest went into the innermost sanctuary and simply breathed.

In the details of the innermost chamber of the wilderness tabernacle, we read that "the cherubim shall have their wings spread out above, shielding the cover with their wings. They shall confront each other...." They gaze at one another, but, even more important, they gaze through the emptiness between them, accentuating the formlessness of God. Here we are at the very center, the holy of holies. And, as anyone who has ever visited an ancient Near Eastern temple knows, that is the residence of the deity. But for the Jews, there is nothing.

Confront each other
Exodus 25:20.

For the Jews, there is nothing
I am grateful to Professor Bernard Horn for this image.

Just as the temple surrounds the holy of holies, the six days of creation serve as a temporal edifice surrounding the Sabbath. Some have suggested that Adam is the High Priest who enters the Sabbath (the holy of holies in time) with one commandment, "but as for the tree of knowledge of good and bad, you must not eat of it...." Creation has at its center an empty throne in an empty room in which the unpronounceable Name is spoken once a year. And the sound of its name is the sound of breathing!

The tree of knowledge
Genesis 2:17.

One of my Bat Mitzvah students, upon hearing that the letters of the *tetragramaton* were all vowels, and therefore

First sound a newborn
Hollis Kramer, Rabbi's Torah Class, January 22, 1989, Congregation Beth El, Sudbury, MA.

were pronounced like breathing and screaming, suggested that the first sound a newborn infant makes as it brings itself into being might be the Name of God.

ONLY NOTHING is GUARANTEED

The opposite of nothing is something. Life is filled with things. And every thing is surrounded by a boundary line separating it from other things. One thing after another is bounded by beginnings and ends, definitions and preconceptions. But only Nothing can embrace all being, infinite possibility, and, therefore, the presence of God. For this reason, one who expects nothing has no guarantees, just openness to every possibility.

Nothing can embrace all
"Wherever there is something there is also another something: every It borders on other Its.... Whoever says [Thou] does not have something; he has nothing."
Martin Buber, *I and Thou*, trans. Walter Kaufmann (New York: Scribners, 1970), 55.

We forget that infinite rebirth is only as far away as Nothing. Dov Baer taught that there can be no change from one form into another without first attaining Nothingness. An egg must first cease to exist as an egg before the chick emerges. So also with everything in the world.

What enormous courage to enter the Nothing of limitless possibility and no guarantees. To let go of the old tangible self, the ego idol, definition, boundary and enter the Nothing. All on the gamble that what you sense within might come to fruition through your courage. To simply entrust yourself to your source. Something akin to exhaling. And about that far away.

As an egg
Rabbi Dov Baer of Mezritch, *Maggid Devarav Leyaakov*, ed. Rivka Schatz-Uffenheimer (Jerusalem: Hebrew University / Magnes Press, 1976), 49. no. 30 (Hebrew); Buber, *The Early Masters*, 104.

Openness to every possibility is dangerous. From a place without limits not only is anything possible but everything is permitted. We must therefore ensure that the Presence of God is neither abused nor defiled. We create religion to protect God, and us, from ourselves. We literally would fall apart in a limitless universe. Unable to endure the anxiety of an empty throne, we panic and turn the Holy No thing into some idolatrous any thing. Sometimes a wood or stone fetish, other times even the very religious system itself.

Some choice: A no-name God, who has no body, on an unknown mountain, in the middle of an empty wilderness, or a tangible, solid, golden calf you could at least see and pet. Do not read *"Moshe boshaysh laredet"* as, "Moses delayed to come down the mountain," but, "Moses was ashamed to come down," because he had no more to show the people of Israel than when he went up. Forty days and all he could say was, "Look at your fingers. Count them. They will remind you how to behave if you hope to endure the terrifying reality that the true Holy One of all being has no home, no body, and no name—only boundless Nothing." No wonder Aaron (who was the other side of Moses' psyche) consented to make us the calf.

Moses was ashamed
Exodus 32:1.

Again and again we trade infinite wonder for a handful of statue; we barter the limitless Nothing for the short-term bird in the hand. And when the deal is done, we have become what we serve: things rather than children of light.

NOW YOU SEE IT, NOW YOU DON'T

In one of the classic perceptual puzzles, we are shown line drawings of three isometric cubes and asked whether they are concave or convex. After rearranging the shadows on the diagram, we realize that they could be either, and with a little concentration, we are able to switch back and forth at will. To our great frustration, we find that we cannot see them simultaneously. We are able to make the image switch between concave and convex through the smallest

[101]

imaginable perceptual shift. But we cannot see something and nothing at the same time. The presence of God is attainable the same way: easily, surprisingly, and, with a little practice, without any effort.

Black fire
Midrash
Tanhuma,
ed. Solomon
Buber, 1.1.

According to Midrash *Tanhumma,* God showed Moses a Torah of black fire written on white fire. The negative ground on and by which all things can be read is itself a message. (I remember, as a rabbinic student, how whenever we complained about the length of a reading assignment, one of our professors would tell us we had only to read the black letters—presumably the white ones would come later.) Every something that is exists within a larger Nothing that is everywhere.

**Function
of our
perception**
The Seer of
Lublin said,
"The Jews
hoped that
God would
dwell among
them on
account of
the taber-
nacle (which I
assume means
organized
religion) but
God longed to
actually dwell
in each per-
son's body and
soul." *Itturay
Torah,* 4:48.

Every "something" has boundaries and limits. You cross them, you're out. But Nothing is always there, right where you are. You don't need to be anywhere or possess anything; you don't even need to put forth your hand. When we say that God is everywhere, we do not mean some invisible, ubiquitous "thing" but another perpetually coexistent mode of being that can be summoned with even casual spiritual discipline. God's presence is a function of our perception. When we realize that every something—our books, our homes, our fears, our friendships, our selves—rests in Nothing, we have entered the Presence.

A LITTLE ROMANCE

In Song of Songs, the unnamed lover (whom we believe to be God) peers at us from behind the lattice of the everyday world. Most of the time we are too preoccupied with our selves to notice. Commenting on the passage in

Deuteronomy, "I stood between the Lord and You," Rabbi Mikhal of Zlotchov said:

Between the Lord and You
Deuteronomy 5:5.

> The "I" stands between God and us. When a person says "I" and encroaches upon the word of God, one puts a wall between oneself and God. But one who offers one's "I," there is nothing between this person and God. For it is to such a one that the words refer: "I am my beloved's and his desire is toward me." When my "I" has become my beloved's, then it is toward me that my beloved's desire turns.

I am my beloved's
Song of Songs 7:11.

His desire turns
Buber, The Early Masters, 149.

Real love means that self-fulfillment comes from forgetting yourself and serving another. Love persuades us to regard ourselves as nothing. To set another's self as more important than our own is mysteriously gratifying. We give our selves away. For this reason, Dov Baer's idea that we must make our selves as nothing and the experience of loving are identical.

Living in "the presence of God" does not mean that we have lost self-awareness; we are just too busy being alive to bother reflecting on ourselves. We are so focused on living that we do not have any leftover awareness to remind us that we exist. We are not aware that we are doing anything, because all our consciousness—even the part reserved for self-reflection—is busy being alive. We are so fully present, unbounded, and un-self-aware that we are not even aware we are present.

The DETAILS of the TABERNACLE

The intricacy of God's instructions for building the wilderness tabernacle, as reported in the later chapters of Exodus, used to puzzle me. God says, "I want so many boards, so many poles, with gold here and precious stones there, all arranged just as I show you." Not only do these plans obviate any human creativity, the myriad explicit details are punctilious beyond anything (except perhaps sacrifices) found anywhere in the Hebrew Bible. A possible clue to understanding the intention here comes from reading the instructions within the context of a love relationship.

When my wife and I were first married, for example, we believed that our "true love" enabled us to read one another's minds. Based on this youthful fantasy, we spent great amounts of time and energy choosing the wrong birthday presents for one another, each pretending we loved gifts we didn't.

As we grew older and our love matured, we gradually realized that even great love only rarely penetrates another's soul. Indeed, I suspect, real loving stands reverent precisely in the mystery of another's unknowable, unfathomable self. And so, as an act of love, we reached a mutual, unspoken decision: We began to drop not-so-subtle hints about what we really wanted. This not only made shopping easier ("This is exactly what she wants!") but receiving presents became much more fun ("Why this is exactly what I wanted!") If you really love someone, don't make them guess what to give you.

Perhaps the relationship between God and the people of Israel is similar. Because God loves us and wants to spare us the inevitable pain of not getting the right present, God tells us exactly how to build the tabernacle.

SECRET AGENTS

In the middle of the night my wife, who is seven months pregnant with our second child, wakes me and whispers, "I know it's the middle of the night, but I would so much love a chocolate bar—preferably one with peanuts." I take on this mission as an honor. My anxiety is not the lost sleep, but that I will not be able to locate the right candy bar. For the better part of an hour, I drive past closed stores until I remember the candy machine at the Holiday Inn. During all this time, I do not have a self of my own. I am my wife's agent. My pleasure comes from ignoring my self, losing my self. How strange and chastening to realize that by serving another self, your self can be so fulfilled.

Through everything we do, we can be agents of God, helping to realize God's plan. We do not forfeit our freedom or our responsibility. Like Abraham's servant, Eliezer, seeking a wife for Isaac, we are messengers on a sacred mission, back in the land of our master's birth. Our mission bestows even trivial acts with great significance. Joseph Weiss, in his classic essay, "Via Passiva in Early Hasidism," teaches that "the mystic becomes an instrument on which God exercises God's exclusive activity. [The mystic] is required to reflect on his actions as nothing but the work of God through him as a medium...."

> **Through him as a medium**
> Weiss, "Via Passiva," 84.

In Mezritch people were said to be like *shofarot* or ram's horns! Just as a *shofar* can make no sound unless breath is blown through, so too people can only say prayers because God moves within them. When we pray, we choose to be a vessel for words that flow through all creation with or without

> **Unless breath is blown**
> *Maggid Devarav Leyaakov*, 184, no. 106.

[105]

our consent. We give them a voice. Arthur Green and Barry Holtz, speaking of Hasidic prayer, observe:

> One should be so absorbed in prayer
>> that one is no longer
>> aware of one's own self.
> There is nothing for such a person
>> but the flow of Life;
>> all one's thoughts are with God.
> One who still knows how intensely one is praying
>> has not yet overcome the bonds of self.

The bonds of self
Arthur Green and Barry W. Holtz, eds., *Your Word Is Fire: The Hasidic Masters on Contemplative Prayer* (New York: Paulist Press, 1977), 55.

MY I, I DID NOT KNOW

Tiferet Shelomo, a Hasidic commentary on the Bible, explains that when Jacob said, "Surely God was in this place and as for me, I did not know," it means: "My I, i did not know. I obliterated everything that was in me; my sense of self-awareness; any consciousness of ego; any trace of self intention. Everything was now only for the sake of the Holy Name itself; for the sake of unifying the holiness within all being and its presence!"

Unifying the holiness
Itturay Torah, 2:257.

Not egotism but self-reflection is the enemy. This is because being in the presence of God, by definition, requires all our awareness—especially and including that part of awareness we ordinarily set just over our shoulder to tell the rest of us that it's us. Self-reflection, in other words, prohibits awareness of God. Dov Baer said:

The work of the pious
Talmud tractate *Ketuvot* 5a.

The work of the pious is greater than the creation of the heavens and the earth. For while the creation of the heavens and the earth was making *something* from nothing, the pious transform something into

[106]

Nothing. Through everything that they do, even with mundane acts like eating, they raise the holy sparks which are within the food back to heaven. And thus with everything they do, they transform something into *Nothing*.

Something into *Nothing*
Maggid Devarav Leyaakav, 24, no. 9.

"It's not that I was selfish. The reason that I didn't know God was here is because I was aware of myself," Jacob muttered.

"And who was it just now who spoke those words," asked the master. (It was a trick question.)

"If someone with the name of 'I' were to answer," mused Jacob out loud, "then surely that person would be aware that it was he who was speaking, and then he would fail the test."

"But of course," smiled Dov Baer. "He would have missed the whole point, indeed."

אכן יש ה' במקום הזה ואנכי לא ידעתי

I could have climbed this ladder of history

5 / NACHMANI

HISTORY

He was well-tailored. His clothes were neither stylish nor expensive, they just fit him well. No one dresses that way by accident. Perhaps he felt he needed an edge because he was short.

Shmuel bar Nachmani Palestine, ca. late 3rd and early 4th centuries CE.

"Here," reasoned Jacob, "is a man who wishes he were taller, more important, more powerful, someone else. Anyone, just someone else." And like so many who feel "destined for the top," this messenger was focused not so much on God but on how to get there. Whenever he wanted to get close to God, he kept bumping into history.

We know, as matter of historical record, that Shmuel bar Nachmani (*bar* is Aramaic for "son of") was a renowned Palestinian rabbinic sage who lived during the late third and early fourth centuries. We know further that he was a native of Lydda, or Lod, on the coastal plain, roughly ten miles southeast of present-day Tel Aviv and home to Ben Gurion Airport. We know also that, as a prominent Jewish leader, he made official visits to Babylon. And, since the Talmud and Midrash preserve the text of many of his teachings, we also can say with certainty that he was a gifted and creative storyteller. Consider the following.

Visits to Babylon
Encyclopedia Judaica, s. v. "Samuel ben Nahman."

This LADDER is a CALENDAR

"Do you see that ladder?" asked the sage. "The higher you go, the more important you are, the longer your political power survives. And those angels ascending and descending, they represent the nations of the world."

Rabbi Shmuel bar Nachmani taught that the Holy One showed Jacob the prince of Babylonia ascending seventy rungs [years]; the prince of Persia ascending fifty-two rungs; the prince of Greece ascending one-hundred-and-eighty rungs; and the prince of Rome ascending more than Jacob could count. When he saw this, Jacob became frightened and asked: "Is it possible that Rome will never come down?"

Jacob, My servant
Isaiah 44:2; Jeremiah 30:10.

The Holy One replied by quoting Scripture, "'Don't be afraid, O' Jacob, My servant,' for even if he ascends all the way to the top and sits beside Me, I will bring him down from there. 'Though you [Edom] make your nest as high as the eagle, and though you set it among the stars, I will bring you down from there.'"

As high as the eagle
Obadiah 1:4.

Rabbi Meir, a contemporary of Nachmani, also taught that the Holy One quoted the same verse to Jacob, "'Don't be afraid, O' Jacob, My servant,' if you ascend the ladder, you will never go down." But Jacob did not believe God and did not ascend. Whereupon the Holy One said to him: "If only you had believed and come up, you never would have come down. Now, however, since you did not believe and did not come up, your children will be enslaved by these four empires."

A contemporary of Nachmani
Midrash *Leviticus Rabba* 29.2. Another version from Midrash *Tanhuma, Vayetze* 2. "According to Rabbi Helvo and Rabbi Shmuel ben Yosayna, God invites Jacob to ascend, but Jacob, fearful of having to come back down like all the others, declines. Even after God reassures him, Jacob is still afraid. In the words of the Midrash, 'He did not believe and he did not ascend.' God said, 'If only you would have gone up, you never would have had to go down! But since you didn't believe, your descendants will serve these four nations....'" Midrash *Exodus Rabba* 32.7; Midrash *Pesikta DeRab Kahana* 23; Midrash *Yalkut Shimoni, Vayetze* 121, *Yermiah* 312.

Bar Nachmani straightened his tie. "It's not that you have been a liar and a cheat; it's not even that you don't trust God; you're just a coward!"

"But I was afraid."

"Of course you were, but it doesn't matter. Fear must never be an excuse. You can be weak, you can be confused, you can even be in prison, but you cannot be afraid. The political forces that seek your acquiescence are counting on you to be afraid. Your fear is their most powerful weapon. And when you refuse to be afraid, they fall from the ladder, they cease to exist."

"Then I will climb it right now," responded Jacob.

"It's too late, the dream is done, and the ladder pulled back up to Heaven."

"Do I ever get another chance?"

"Probably. There most likely will be hundreds of ladders. But they don't come with signs saying, 'I am a ladder, don't be afraid, climb me now.' If they did, we would all be heroes, bravely seizing each historic moment, bringing history closer to God."

FLEEING HISTORY

He is afraid precisely because he is running away, not just from his brother, Esau, but from his parents and everything that he has been. And, as Nachmani's interpretation of the ladder suggests, Jacob is also running away from history. He does not want to take responsibility for his life or his world or to enter either as an active participant. Until now he has lived out his mother's dreams or simply done what she told him. He tricked his brother and his father (and will trick Laban, his brother-in-law) into giving him what he wants. In the future he will return to this same place, again at night and alone, and God will come to him once more. And he will finally reenter his past as a man. But that will take another twenty years, and last night's dream is only the beginning. So it is not the least bit surprising that he declined God's present offer to step onto the ladder.

His grandfather and even his father were different.

ENTERING HISTORY

They both stood
Midrash
Genesis Rabba
55.7.

"Your grandfather, Abraham, and your father, Isaac, they both stood on this spot. And they 'stepped up to the plate,' as the saying goes. Abraham and Isaac initiated history

[112]

when they decided to follow God's command. Because of their merit in stepping forward, your relationship with God is now assured. Now God asks you to ascend the ladder, but you are afraid."

"But I didn't realize that *this* moment was history. I thought it was just another ordinary moment. I didn't realize that One other than me was also watching, waiting, hoping, peering through the lattice. I didn't think that I could have any impact, that what I did or did not do mattered."

"Well realize it now: What people do matters. Either human actions are connected to what happens in the universe, or they are not. And if everything is connected to everything else, then sooner or later everything matters; everything is potentially historic. We are already *of* history. That is what you can learn from what Abraham and Isaac did on Mount Moriah. They did not simply do what they heard God say. They trusted where God had put them and in what God put before them. They chose to step forward into their destiny."

Because of their merit As we shall see in the last chapter, rabbinic tradition imagines that Isaac was a willing participant in the whole drama.

Peering through the lattice Song of Songs 2:9.

VORKI on JEWISH SURVIVAL

According to one Hasidic tradition, Isaac of Vorki taught that the real test of Abraham's devotion to God was not merely that he consented to follow God's command. "After all," he asks, "just what did Abraham do that was such a big deal? He was an ordinary human being, a simple Jew, and the God of the whole universe appears to him with a request. Who wouldn't fulfill such a command? Refusing or even thinking it over for a while are simply out of the question. No, the real test came in a conversation Abraham had with Satan. Satan said, 'Abraham, look at what you're about to do. Ishmael, the son you had with Hagar, is already irretrievably lost to Judaism. That leaves only two Jewish men in the entire world: you and Isaac. So now do the simple arithmetic. You and Sarah are old; you will have no more children. If you go and slaughter your son Isaac, you will literally blot out Jewish men from the universe!' But Abraham our father," explains Isaac of Vorki, "would hear none of these arguments. Instead he replied, 'My job is to do what God wants. Whether or not the world has Jews is God's business, not mine!'"

God's
business,
not mine
Itturay Torah,
1:159.

REMEMBER, YOU WERE A SLAVE

There are many ways to confront history. Some people are *Luftmenschen* (sky people), living beyond history in hermit retreats or in the theological clouds of other worlds waiting for God. Others try to be *Ubermenschen* (super people), grabbing history by the throat and drinking its life blood for their own power and vainglory. But not Jews. They get neither peace nor power; instead, they must be *"Gründmenschen"* (grounded people), ones stuck with barely enough power to survive on this earth. Their survival is not ensured by seeking it but rather in accord with one principle: Remember, once you were a slave. You know deep inside what it is like to be a stranger, other, powerless.

Prohibition
against
oppressing
Nehama
Leibowitz,
*Studies in
the Weekly
Parasha*
(Jerusalem:
World Zionist
Organization,
1962–80),
2:380.

In one way or another, this biblical prohibition against oppressing the stranger is reiterated in no less than thirty-six different forms. No other commandment—including loving God, observing Sabbath, or refraining from forbidden foods—is invoked so many times. We therefore are not surprised to learn that the Passover feast, the *seder* meal celebrating our freedom and reminding us that once we too were slaves, remains the most widely observed Jewish holiday. Even Jews who claim they are no longer Jews have a big dinner on the eve of the fifteenth of the spring lunar month of *Nisan*. They eat no leavened bread; instead they eat only *matzah*, the unleavened bread of slaves. They remember they once were slaves.

Before this imageless God of the Hebrew Bible was willing to assign the Jewish people a mission, God insisted they experience political powerlessness and social disenfranchisement. They must never forget. Indeed, as sociologist Milton Himmelfarb once quipped, Jews live like Episcopalians but vote like Puerto Ricans!

Milton Himmelfarb
Leonard Fein, *Where Are We? The Inner Life of America's Jews* (New York: Harper & Row, 1988), 225.

RUNNING CONVERSATION

How ironic. Nothing happens in the lifetime of this God of the Jews. Indeed, there is no lifetime. This God knows neither birth nor death, neither marries nor bears children, was never young, never grows old. In a word, this God has no mythology. So not only does God have neither an image nor a pronounceable Name, God also has no personal history. And yet, one of Judaism's most radical insights into the human condition is that events of history happen only once. They do not recur. Time only flows forward.

Prior to this, religious thought assumed that time eternally circled back upon itself, over and over again. Every event—not just birth, marriage, and death, but kings, famines, wars, and peace—drew its reality from participation in eternal mythic archetypes. God, like any other king, also was captive to these cycles.

The Hebrew Bible came along and said that God didn't work like that. What makes God God is that God began the flow of time "In the beginning" and continues to move mysteriously within time in such a way as to give us human actors a big say in how things are going to turn out, and, at some undisclosed future, God will bring time to an end.

The Hebrew Bible taught that things "came to pass." Sooner or later, sometimes very much later, wicked rulers and their nations would be assigned an evaluation by an absolute measure. This standard, God's standard, endures from generation to generation. It has many versions—different dialects—but there is no minority position that permits maltreatment of widows or orphans or slaves. And how they are treated is the baseline of human history. While God may have no personal history, human beings and their nations do. And human beings and God, says the Hebrew Bible (and especially its prophets), carry on a conversation through the nonrepeatable events of history.

GOD'S MORNING PAPER

Jewish historiography
Yosef Hayim Yerushalmi, Zakhor: Jewish History and Jewish Memory (Seattle: University of Washington Press, 1982), 11.

The historian Yosef Yerushalmi, writing of Jewish historiography, observes that "… above all, God's acts of intervention in history, and our responses to them, be they positive or negative … must be recalled." They are the substance of history.

But how do we know which events are significant? We are confronted with a daily barrage of often conflicting political data. What once seemed to be trivial, turns out to have been important. What once was a headline, now is irrelevant. Even possessing all the facts only confuses. Without a meaning system in which to put them, we do not know which pieces are important.

History may be understood as the flow of human events viewed from some independent value system that gives them importance, purpose, direction, significance, meaning. Without a model for history, events, lives, and ideas are all equally important and unimportant, relevant and irrelevant. But with some transcendent measure, we are able to comprehend the significance and meaning of our lived experience. To have history requires something beyond history. And for the Hebrew Bible, what we call history is how we imagine the sequence of human decisions recounted in the morning paper looks to God. And when we read about them while trying to imagine how they might appear to God, we realize the significance of our decisions and the events they shape.

LUXURY of EXILE

For Jews in the second half of the twentieth century, the question of history is focused on Zionism. In its simplest form, the Holocaust was the result of the Jews' refusal (or inability) to climb the ladder, to enter history, and to control their own destiny. And the State of Israel is the result of the Jews' decision to leave the powerlessness of exile—living in someone else's country—and enter history. Living for nearly two millennia on the fringe of history, in exile, may have given us a keen sensitivity to the social disenfranchisement of others but left us politically anomalous and unable to protect ourselves. The State of Israel, the Zionists claim, would both protect Jews and make them normal once again. The Jews of the American exile, unwilling to "come home," counter that we don't want to be normal nor do we want to be judged by a normal standard of political behavior. (This may explain the "double standard" by which the American press frequently judges Israel.) Zionism replies that the choice is between the luxury of moral powerlessness and the burden of justly exercising real political power. (Since the argument has gone on throughout most of Jewish history, we do not anticipate a conclusion in the near future.)

"The Diaspora Syndrome: Cause and Cure," Congregation Beth El, Sudbury, MA, May 7, 1988.

A. B. Yehoshua, one of Zionism's most creative teachers, once observed that the first thing Abraham did when he arrived in Israel was to leave. (In returning to Haran, Jacob also is leaving the land. Which side of the border was the site of his dream? This is no trivial matter, since some argue that divine visions can *only* occur *within* the land of Israel itself.) Yehoshua says that Abraham, the first Jew, went down to Egypt, presaging the great exile. And the first thing Abraham did when he arrived in Egypt was tell the Egyptians that Sarah, his wife, was his sister. In other words, adds Yehoshua, "to be in exile means you must lie." The implication is clear: Jews who live outside the land of Israel cannot be players in history. Deprived of the possibility of serious political action, they, like all non-players, are condemned instead to lie, manipulate, coax, and connive.

Sarah, his wife
Genesis 12:13.

American Jews retort that their lobby continues to guarantee the United States' support for Israel. Furthermore, one can argue that since the destruction of the first and second temples, and even the devastating loss of the Bar Kochba rebellion, happened while the Jewish people had a state, and the expulsion from Spain, the Khelmnitsky massacres, and the Holocaust happened while we did not, the quality of "statedness" has little bearing on the physical security of the Jewish people. Whatever it is that enables the Jewish people to survive does not seem to be affected by the existence of a Jewish state. One thing is certain. With or without a state, Jews, like Jacob, must step up onto the ladder. Serious religion means politics.

CHANGING PLANES

Perhaps you have had the experience of changing planes in some distant airport. All an airline's flights converge on what the airline calls a "hub" city, and about an hour later they all leave again. During that hour, passengers have enough time (usually) to get off one plane and onto another. This ingenious system enables the maximum number of people to go to the most cities with the minimum of airplanes. From this hub airport, during this hour, one can go almost anywhere. But if your plane arrives late, you can go nowhere. Everything depends upon this hour, this convergence, this "window." It is the same way with history.

There are moments of seemingly enormous historic significance, times when the confluence of political forces and one's own power create the potential for sudden change, windows of opportunity. Unfortunately, we usually only realize the presence of such opportunities in retrospect. "If I had only known then...." And so it goes. Like Jacob who didn't realize until he awoke that God had really been present and that a ladder had joined heaven and earth. At that time, Nachmani suggests, anything might have been possible.

In the same way that God's presence can be anywhere and anytime, so too any act may be historic. One vote can change the result of an election, a joke at the right moment can change the course of a meeting, anywhere and anytime the most otherwise trivial gesture can and does have world-historic consequences. But we rarely realize the effect until too late. It is incumbent upon us to remember that each moment can be decisive and therefore historic.

WHO IS TO SAY?

There was
this kid
*Encyclopedia
Judaica*, s. v.
"Samuel bar
Nahman."

"Once," confessed Shmuel bar Nachmani, "when I was already an old man, I went to Babylonia. By this time in my life I was important, a leader. And there was this kid, an orphan, who committed some grave political crime. To tell the truth, I don't even remember what it was. But I took myself all the way to Babylon and pleaded with the Empress Zenobia herself to pardon him. I remember feeling frightened and thinking that I was doing something important. She let the kid off. If I hadn't gone, he surely would have been executed."

"That was very brave and very important," agreed Jacob. "Still, it's hard to tell. For all you know, just showing me how the ladder in my dream represents history could also change history."

"But that is impossible," answered bar Nachmani. "You didn't even climb the ladder."

"That's true. But what if I share the image with one of my children, who in turn shares it with still another generation. Someone, someday might write it in a book, and someone else might read it and copy it into still another. And people who did not know either one of us might read the story. Just think of it. Thousands of years from now, the parable of some second-century Palestinian sage still read and studied. Surely that also could have real historic significance."

Into the SEA on DRY GROUND

While working with a class of ten-year-olds in preparation for Passover, I was asked whether or not miracles really happen. Since Cecil B. DeMille's *The Ten Commandments* had been on television the night before, the question was transparent. The spiritual damage the film has done to a generation of children is enormous. That tradition is compelled to put into words what cannot be put into words is bad enough. Now Hollywood literalizes them into static images. Whenever you see the movie, it is always the same. The biblical text says, for example, that the waters of the Red Sea "stood like walls." The movie depicts literal walls. The mystery is gone. One wonders whether the original prohibition of making any likeness of God should not apply also to miracles or, for that matter, to anything sacred.

Stood like walls Exodus 15:8.

Far more appropriate is the rabbinic preoccupation with the logical impossibility of walking "into the midst of the sea on dry ground." Either it is dry ground, in which case you are not walking into the midst of the sea, or it is the sea, in which case it cannot be dry ground. The children naturally were trying to integrate such a preposterous scene into the world in which they lived. And I was trying to save a few of them for religious tradition. To stonewall would have been easy, but instead I told them the story of Reuven and Shimon who were so preoccupied with the mud on the sea bed that, even though they walked through the "miracle," they never noticed it. I hoped, in this way, at least to leave the question open.

Midst of the sea Exodus 14:16, 22, 29, 15:19; Nehemiah 9:11.

But one of the children raised the ante. She correctly reminded me that crossing through the split sea was the way the Jewish people became free. (You had to walk to freedom on the distant shore to participate in your own creation as a free man or woman.) Does this mean that Reuven and Shimon, even though they "made it to the other side," were not really free? Before I could think of an answer, someone else quickly deduced that "seeing miracles" was the only way to get free. "So that's who God is," I thought, "the One who is

Only way to get free I am grateful to Catherine Cogley for this insight.

[121]

the source of freedom. And our ability to be free is a function of our ability to see miracles, our willingness to step into the midst of the sea on dry ground."

FEMININE HISTORY

Men and women make sense
Deborah Tannen, *You Just Don't Understand: Women and Men in Conversation* (New York: William Morrow, 1990), 25.

Deborah Tannen writes of the differing ways in which men and women make sense of and describe their lives. Her observations may also be relevant to our own understanding of history. A man, or the generically masculine, engages the world, Tannen notes, "as an individual in a hierarchical social order in which he [is] either one-up or one-down.... Life, then, is a contest, a struggle to preserve independence and avoid failure."

But a woman ... engages the world "as an individual in a network of connections.... [Women] try to protect themselves from others' attempts to push them away. Life, then, is a community, a struggle to preserve intimacy and avoid isolation."

In light of Tannen's observations, we realize that most of what we learn as history is told in masculine metaphors. Power, control, who is "up" and who is "down." Even Nachmani's image of the ladder seems unmistakably masculine. But here too the Midrash offers another perspective.

Standing at Jacob's side
Midrash *Genesis Rabba* 69.1–3.

The text of Jacob's dream says, "And behold a ladder and ... God is standing on it." Noting that the Hebrew for "on it," *alav* can also mean "by him," the Midrash suggests that God was standing at Jacob's side while he dreamt. In this vision of history, hierarchical position is not nearly as important as relationship.

God (we imagine) says, "Let the nations fight with one another for who can be top dog. Such is not your destiny. So do not be afraid, Jacob. I am with you, not to insure moral superiority but to heighten moral sensitivity." And Jacob awoke.

HANDS of GOD

The last attempt at democratic reform in China ended in Tiananmen Square. In retrospect, the live video image of a lone student momentarily stopping a tank by standing in front of it captures more than a solitary confrontation. It portrays more than courage in the face of overwhelming odds. The image does not go away. That particular young person, alas, may have perished, but that particular image will not leave us until all the tanks have gone. I wonder what he was thinking? What happened before the video was taken? What was the midrashic subtext that led to that moment, no longer than a sound byte? Had he joined his friends from college and been swept into the moment? Was he a leader of the revolution? Perhaps a farmer who came to the city, drawn by the optimism of those extraordinary weeks? Did the times make the person, or did the person make the times?

As recently as a year ago one could pay to have someone smuggled across the border into illegal sanctuary in the United States in order to save that person from Salvadorian death squads. It was called the "coyote price." Such a life sold for around $1,600.

Often the window through which you can alter history is as ordinary as a stranger coming to your door and asking for food or money. Other times a tank appears on the street, and you must decide whether or not you will stand in its path. But whether as easy as giving a few dollars or as terrifying as putting your life in jeopardy, something is laid before you. There are many ways to avoid action. We blame others, we say the problem is too big or too complicated, we close our eyes, we tell lies. But finally we are free only to step into this moment or back away from it. No matter what we do or do not do, we have made our decision.

If a person who cynically refused to believe in God could observe everything a congregation said and did whenever its members gathered for prayer, study, and communal meetings, by the end of a year or two he would know a lot about what God does, even if God never showed up. For, while God does not have hands, we do. Our hands are God's. And when people behave as if their hands were the hands of God, then God "acts" in history.

MYTH and HISTORY

Just as historians are divided over whether people make the times or the times make the people, there are two modes of religious response to history. They appear in every religious tradition. Our inclination to choose one or the other is a function more of personality than of reasoned theology. Judaism certainly has both. Think of them as two ways of understanding reality. One mode is myth, the other history.

Writing of myth, Yosef Yerushalmi observes:

In primitive societies, only mythic rather than historical time is "real." ... The present, historical moment ... achieves meaning and reality only by subverting itself, when through the repetition of a ritual or the recitation or re-enactment of a myth, historical time is periodically shattered and one can experience again, if only briefly, the true time of the origins and archetypes....

Thus in a mythic conception of time, everything continually recurs in the lifetime of each human being. A myth is a metahistorical story that happens over and over again. One who encounters the myth leaves nonrepeatable history for a more primary reality. The transformation of slaves into free women and men by passing through the Red Sea, the wandering in the wilderness and receiving of the Torah, the leaving of the garden of Eden, such mythic events happen generation after generation in the life of each person. Though the story may not have happened in precisely the way narrated, it is true in a psycho-spiritual sense. With myth there are no surprises; what has been will be again. The names of the characters and their costumes will vary from one situation to the next, but the essentials of the mythic drama reappear unchanged. They lie beneath each apparently novel event as a matrix, an underlying reality. Things will end the way they began.

In contradistinction to the security and predictability of myth is the anxiety of freedom, the chastening of linear time's irreversibility. The events of history do not recur. They happen only once. And humanity is free to affect them. In the prophetic religion of the later books of the Hebrew Bible, human decisions and actions become the sources of surprise. Each discrete act is our response to the God of history. Our actions have profound and unrepeatable significance. Reading the morning paper becomes a religious act, for it sets the agenda of what must be repaired this day.

Origins and archetypes
Yerushalmi, *Zakhor*, 6–7; Mircea Eliade, *The Myth of Eternal Return, or Cosmos and History*, trans. Willard Trask (Princeton: Princeton University Press, 1954), 34–48; Mircea Eliade, *The Sacred and the Profane: The Nature of Religion*, trans. Willard Trask (New York: Harcourt, Brace & World, 1959), ch. 2.

[125]

But there is a paradox here. The great, decisive moments of history, the truly once-in-a-lifetime moments, have an unmistakably mythic aura. The more decisive or apparently nonrepeatable the moment, the more mythic and eternal it seems to be.

In history the self is unable to be one with God because the space separating them is an abyss. In *devekut*, the mystic union, the divine self and the individual are momentarily one, and since at such a moment everything appears as precisely the way it is supposed to be, goals, improvements, repair, and even action itself are unnecessary and effectively impossible.

How then could Jacob have a mystical experience, a dream of this ladder joining heaven and earth in which he is invited by God to ascend the ladder, and effectively end the moment of mystic union with God?

Sun cycle
The sun was created on Tuesday, coinciding with the vernal equinox. But since the solar year is 52 weeks and 1 1/4 days, the sun will not pass the celestial equator moving north again for another 28 years. The *Birkat HaHama*, blessing the sun on this occasion is referred to in Talmud tractate *Berakhot* 59b.

ENVIRONMENT as RESOLUTION

Our newly emerging understanding of the environment provides us with a new metaphor for the synthesis of mythic and linear conceptions of history. The environment embodies both. We are all living manifestations of an organism called the environment. And this organism seems to move through daily, weekly, monthly, annual cycles. There are even larger, not immediately evident cycles. Every twenty-eight years, the sun cycle. And there are cycles of forest fire and regeneration. And yet, for all our knowledge of nature's rhythms, we sense an urgency in our present condition. We correctly understand that we can inflict irreversible ecological damage. Whole species can disappear. In the environment the mythic cycles of nature coexist with the irreversibility of linear time.

We must act in ways that will ensure that the ever-renewing web of nature will continue to be spun.

ALL HISTORY at ONCE

Once, when he was a boy, Jacob asked his grandfather Abraham if he had ever had a mystical experience.

"Did you ever see the *merkava* (the chariot of the Divine Presence)? I mean what was it like?"

Chariot of the Divine Presence
Ezekiel, chs. 1, 10.

"Once," replied the old man, "I think I did. I mean, once it was clear to me that I was, how do they say it, face to face, I took your father up on the mountain. What I saw was not awesome or thrilling, just frightening. I was very scared...."

"Did you see a likeness of God, the way Ezekiel did?"

"No, I saw no image that I remember. I saw something that then and now still seems terrifying."

"What did you see?"

"I saw history. I saw our past and our future. Not that our history is so monstrous. Other people have some pretty lousy histories too; it's just that we Jews have so much of it. I saw how our people would endure slavery for four hundred years and how, after all that degradation, God would set us free."

I saw history
"The Covenant Between the Pieces," Genesis 15.

"That sounds pretty good," said the boy.

"I know what you're saying. But I saw it all at once. To see someone a slave, that's terrible. To see someone set free, that's a great joy. To see it all at once, as if from some high, nonexistent mountain in time, that is terrible. It's as if the slavery and the freedom are always present within one another. The joy contains the sadness. The sadness, the joy. You try to untangle them and set each on its own stage so you can have one at a time, but when I saw the chariot, I saw them all superimposed upon one another. I was unable

[127]

to cry, because I knew I would also laugh. I could not feel the joy, for I knew the price that had been paid."

"Did you see the *acharyit*, the End?" the boy asked. "Does it stop, or does it just keep going?"

"To see the *merkava* at any time is to see both the beginning and the end. Unlike the astronomers (who are undecided if there is enough matter in the universe to have it all come collapsing back to one single dimensionless point one day, or whether matter will just go on expanding forever outward into the vacuum), we are convinced. All being conspires to return to one point of light from whence it began, just as now all being is contained in the Holy One.

"Because you and I and all human beings are created in one image, we are, each of us, versions of God. We are to God as the DNA molecule is to us. So, in addition to seeing the beginning and the end, I also saw myself. All was within me. I stood there with my arms and legs stretched out like the rays of the sun and watched all being pass before me. It was all in my hands. I could do with creation whatever I pleased!"

THREE NIGHTS RUNNING

I will be with you
Parasha Vayetze,
Genesis 28:10–32:3.

I will change your name
Parasha Vayishlach,
Genesis 32:4–36:43.

I will redeem you
Parasha Vayigash,
Genesis 44:18–47:27.

Because Jacob's first two nighttime encounters so quickly capture our imagination, we forget that he has three. The first is the ladder dream. God says in it, "I will be with you." The second (which people occasionally confuse with the first) was the wrestling match. God (or whoever it was that wrestled with Jacob) says, "I will change your name." The third comes when Jacob is a man. God says, "I will redeem you in Egypt."

And Israel set out with everything he owned and he came to Beer-sheba, and he offered sacrifices to the

God of his father, Isaac. And God spoke to Israel in a night vision and God said, "Jacob! Jacob!" and he answered, "Here am I." And God said, "I (*Anochi*, אנכי) am God, the God of your father. Do not be afraid to descend into Egypt, for there I will make you a great nation. I Myself will go down with you into Egypt and I Myself will also bring you out; and Joseph's hand shall close your eyes.

Close your eyes Genesis 46:1–4.

The third, and final, nighttime encounter lays a new, ultimate, and historic challenge before Jacob. God calls Jacob's name twice (echoing God's call to Abraham at Moriah and Moses at the burning bush) and Jacob responds with that extraordinary biblical word reserved for unrestrained consent: "*Heneni*, here I am, ready to do whatever needs be done." "Now," says God, "you will have to go down into Egypt. Your foreboding is appropriate but do not be afraid. It is all part of a larger plan. And your favorite son, Joseph, will be with you when you die."

Now Jacob is ready to enter history, to encounter his destiny, to do what needs be done.

From his vantage point high up on the ladder, Shmuel bar Nachmani could see all this of course, but he decided not to tell Jacob. Jacob wouldn't have believed him.

[129]

אכן יש ה' במקום הזה ואנכי לא ידעתי

I is the Lord your God

6 / DE LEÓN

The SELF of the UNIVERSE

Imagine: a long-hidden, second-century manuscript written by Shimon bar Yohai, one of the great visionaries of all time, faithfully handed down through the generations from master to disciple. And imagine more, that copies of selected portions are for sale at a modest price. Maybe you're interested in looking at a few pages?

Such a rumor was more than enough to entice a young Kabbalist named Isaac ben Samuel. Fleeing the Mamaluk invasion of Acre by way of Italy, he came to the northeastern

Moses ben Shem Tov de León
Province of Castile, Spain, ca. 1240–1305.

Spanish province of Castile in 1305. There Isaac learned that the purveyor of these tantalizing folios was one Moses ben Shem Tov de León, whom Isaac finally located in Valladolid. Isaac records the meeting in his diary. Moses promised Isaac that he did indeed possess a copy of the coveted ancient manuscript and that if he would come to Avila, where Moses was now living, he could examine it for himself.

In his diary
Gershom Scholem, *Kabbalah* (New York: Quadrangle, 1974), 432.

But, alas, before Isaac arrived, de León fell ill and died. Saddened but determined, Isaac sought out de León's widow. Not only had the manuscript apparently vanished into thin air, but, the woman swore, it never had even existed. Professor Daniel Matt relates the account in her own words:

> When I saw him writing with nothing in front of him, I said to him, "Why do you say that you are copying from a book when there is no book? You are writing from your head. Wouldn't it be better for you to say so? You would have more honor!"

> He answered me, "If I told them my secret, that I am writing from my own mind, they would pay no attention to my words, and they would pay nothing for them."

They would pay nothing
Matt, *Zohar*, 4.

The following is without any historical evidence whatsoever. "In that case," the unnamed wife of de León replied, "let me help you. If you want to write about God who encompasses the masculine and the feminine dimensions of creation, you will need to listen to the experience of a woman."

I once asked Daniel Matt, who was tutoring me in *Zohar*, why, in the *Zohar's* *sefirotic* diagram purporting to describe the infrastructure of creation with ten spheres arranged in

a male-female, yin-yang balance, mothering was understood as stern and judgmental while fathering was tender
and forgiving. They seemed to reverse human experience.
He thought for a moment and surmised with a smile that
the *Baal HaZohar*, the author of the *Zohar*, must have had
one helluva mother. It occurs to me now that his wife may
have written much of the book. What we do know is that
all Kabbalists, or Jewish mystics, had access to the feminine dimension of themselves and of God. For them, God
was potentially both male and female. I now suspect that, in
some sense, all were women, every last one of them, drawing freely not only from both sides of consciousness but also
from gender.

The BOOK of ENLIGHTENMENT

Moses de León's book was titled the *Zohar*. Actually a
collection of several different commentaries and midrashim
purporting to be a commentary on the Five Books of Moses,
its title means "radiance" or "splendor." And, like all great
works of mysticism, it draws freely from the mother lode of
spirituality: the congruence of God and innermost self. So
intricate and fertile was this "Book of Enlightenment" that,
by the sixteenth century, not only had the *Zohar* become the
central text of Jewish mysticism but, as Matt observes, it also
ranked in importance next to the Talmud itself!

Only a few decades ago, through the meticulous, philo-
logical research of the late historian Gershom Scholem, was
proof of de León's authorship conclusively established. Nevertheless, to this day among faithful, traditional Jews, the
author of the *Zohar* is still Shimon bar Yohai. Perhaps they
each shared the same soul.

[133]

ANOTHER NAME for GOD

De León was gentle yet (we must assume) mischievous, world-renouncing but in love with all things that smelled and tasted good. His eyes were always wide open, not glassy or penetrating, just wide awake as if he were always seeing things for the first time. (In the Talmud, it is said of Shimon bar Yohai that his gaze was so intense that on one occasion whatever he saw was incinerated.)

Gaze was so intense Talmud tractate *Shabbat* 33b.

"Let me explain," offered de León. "Last night you learned something new about God...."

Jacob second-guessed the wrong answer: "I learned that God was with me even in a desolate place."

"No, you knew that already. You learned something much more intimate about God. You learned a new Name."

"God was in this place," Jacob rehearsed the verse, "and I, i did not know. There's no new Name there."

"Do you remember how Kotzk and Mezritch called your attention to that redundant 'I'?"

"Yes," he replied.

"Well, they were on to something, but they didn't take it far enough. Suppose one of the *I*'s doesn't refer to your ego or another mode of consciousness; suppose it refers to God. Suppose one of the *I*'s, the first one, is actually another Name for God. What I'm saying is that we know God has many names. The list is probably endless.

"But perhaps there was a Name for God that until last night neither you nor anyone else had ever known before. Suppose one of God's Names is: 'I, *Anochi*, אנכי.' Now the verse reads, 'Surely God was in this place, but by the Name, 'I, *Anochi*, אנכי' i did not know.' Do you understand me?"

The author of the *Zohar*'s eyes were wide open, "God's Name is I, *Anochi*, אנכי!"

God's Name is I "What Jacob really said was: 'And I have not known *Anochi* (I, i.e., the *Shekhinah*)'; as much as to say: 'Behold all this revelation has been vouchsafed to me whilst yet I have not reached the stage of knowledge of *Anochi* (I) and of entering under the wings of the *Shekhinah*, so as to attain perfection.'" *The Zohar*, trans. Harry Sperling and Maurice Simon (New York: Soncino Press, 1933), 2:82.

"Oh, God!" whispered Jacob. "That means that God and I both call ourselves by the same name. And (the logic was simple) if God's Name is I (*Anochi* אנכי) , then God must also have a Self." His mind felt like it suddenly had turned itself inside out.

The WORD WE SHARE with GOD

With the exception of one word, human words and Divine words cannot be the same. Infinite language cannot be mortal speech, except for one word—the first person singular pronoun "I," "*Anochi*, אנכי." For just this is the name each self has for its self. And, since the gesture of self-reference— the way by which I evoke who I am—is the same for every self, whenever we say "I" we evoke not only the "I" of every other soul, we echo the primary "I," "*Anochi*, אנכי," of Sinai. Whatever makes each individual unique, that innermost core self, is precisely what we each share with one another, and with our Creator. We are made of the same holy stuff. It has this mysterious ability to look different in each pair of eyes, to sound different in each voice, but it is all the same.

PRAYING by the OCEAN

Professor Richard Rubenstein of Florida State University offers a classical and elegant explanation of this relationship we have with God.

God is the ocean and we are the waves. In some sense each wave has its moment in which it is distinguishable as a somewhat separate entity. Nevertheless, no wave is entirely distinct from the ocean which is its substantial ground. The waves are surface manifestations of the ocean. Our knowledge of

God is the ocean Richard L. Rubenstein, *Morality and Eros* (New York: McGraw-Hill, 1970), 186–87.

the ocean is largely dependent on the way it manifests itself in the waves.

But you cannot simultaneously be aware that you are the wave *and* be aware that you are part of the ocean. And that is why God is so elusive. In a similar vein, theologian Alan Watts suggests that "God is the self of the world, but you can't see God for the same reason that, without a mirror, you can't see your own eyes...." Consider, for instance, what such an idea would do to our understanding of prayer.

See your own eyes Alan Watts, *The Book: On the Taboo Against Knowing Who You Are* (New York: Collier Books, 1966), 13.

Assuming the waves could speak, what should they say to the ocean? Perhaps the most meaningful noise they could make would be the rhythmic, relentless whisper they make as they rise and fall, come in and out of being. Surely that is a worthy prayer. Surely those prayerful sounds, if they could be scored on paper, would be worthy of regular rehearsal, for they would remind each wave of the source of its being. Making those sounds would remind each wave that it was indeed a wave and, contrary to all the wave's illusions, not something else.

You might say that we have only two options: We can recite the words, acknowledge that we are all waves of the same sea, made of the same stuff, creatures of the same Creator, or we can be too busy to make the words, recite the prayer, offer the service.

We can on occasion, to select another analogy, choose to be aware of the barely audible noise made by the involuntary emptying and filling of our lungs, this noise by which we live. Or we can ignore and take it for granted. The only casualty is our own awareness, our sense of life.

Prayers run in two directions, for the ocean also speaks to the waves. But since the waves are already part of the ocean, their sound is, in some sense, the sound of their source speaking to them. They are the mouth of the ocean, and their prayer is the way the sea has of speaking to itself.

In the same way, the words of the prayerbook and all the meditations of our hearts are the sound of God speaking to God. As Rabbi Kalynomos Kalmish Shapira of Piesetzna, who perished in the Warsaw ghetto, used to say, "Not only does God hear our prayers, God prays them through us as well."

Prays them through us
I am grateful to Dr. Nehemiah Polen for sharing this teaching with me.

Other Hasidim went even further. They equated the one who prays with the very prayer that is offered: "You are your prayer." Until finally prayer, the one who offers it, and the One who hears it are one and the same. Arthur Green and Barry Holtz observe that:

> The worshiper continues to recite the words of prayer, but it is no longer the worshiper who speaks them. Rather it is the Presence who speaks through the worshiper. In that prayerful return to the Source one has reached the highest human state, becoming nought but the passive instrument for the ever self-proclaiming praise of God.

Return to the Source
Green and Holtz, *Your Word Is Fire*, 14.

Imagine that the double helix coil of deoxyribonucleic acid in your genes wanted to speak to the double helix coil of deoxyribonucleic acid in your father and mother. They would only reply, "Why do you speak to us? Does not everything you have and everything you are come from us? Together, we are the source of your uniqueness."

So it is with us and God during prayer. What more is there to say except to acknowledge this primal mystery with ritualized regularity and religious ecstasy. Indeed, for this reason perhaps the only worthwhile conversation is to rehearse routinely that ancient truth morning, afternoon, and evening. "Oh Lord, open my lips that my mouth may declare your praise."

Open my lips
Psalm 51:17.

LOSING YOUR SOUL to the FIRST WORD

If encountering God means loss of self, it is little wonder that our ancestors were so ambivalent at Sinai. If a person got too close, heard too much, he or she might never come back.

Restored their souls
Midrash
Song of Songs Rabba 5.16, iii: Midrash *Exodus Rabba* 29.3.

When the Israelites heard the word "*Anochi,* אנכי," the "I" [of the first word of the ten utterances at Mount Sinai], their souls left them.... The Divine utterance returned to the Holy One and said: "Sovereign of the Universe, You are full of life, and Your Torah is full of life. But You have sent me to the dead. They are all dead!" Thereupon God sweetened the word for them [and made it less powerful]....

Torah of the Lord
Psalm 19:8.

Rabbi Simeon bar Yohai explained that the Torah, which the Holy One then gave to Israel, restored their souls to them. That is why it is said in the Psalm, "The Torah of the Lord is perfect, restoring the soul." It brings us *back* to life.

EVERYTHING in ONE WORD

Hebrew has no verb "to be" in the present tense. This means that there is no way to say "am," "is," or "are" and that any attempt to speak of "being," at least in the present, can be inferred only from context but never spoken. The language creates its own circumlocutions, and Hebrew speakers carry on ordinary lives in the present tense like everyone else. But in the case of the first of the ten utterances at Sinai, we are left with one tantalizing ambiguity.

Those seven Hebrew words translated into literal English are: "I Lord your-God who brought-you from-the-Land-of Egypt." So while they can mean, "I am the Lord, your God...." they can just as easily and properly be rendered, "I (*Anochi*, אנכי) *is* the Lord your God."

Furthermore, according to the Midrash, the passage in Exodus "And God spoke all these words, saying" means that "God spoke all the ten commandments with one utterance." Just think of it: Everything rolled within the seed of the first utterance, I (*Anochi*, אנכי), the Name of God and the source of our own selfhood.

Gershom Scholem recounts a similarly daring legend in the name of Rabbi Mendel Torum of Rymanov.

In Rabbi Mendel's view ... all that Israel heard was the *aleph* ... of the word *Anochi*, אנכי, 'I' ... [and] the consonant *aleph* represents nothing more than the position taken by the larynx when a word begins a vowel. Thus the *aleph* may be said to denote the source of all articulate sound....

But the *Zohar* takes the idea to its ultimate conclusion:

Rabbi Eleazar taught that in the Ten Words (decalogue) all the other commandments were engraved, with all decrees and punishments, all laws concerning

All these words
Exodus 20:1.

With one utterance
Midrash *Numbers Rabba* 11.7.

The First Utterance
Zohar II 85b.

All articulate sound
Scholem, *On the Kabbalah*, 30–31.

[139]

purity and impurity, all the branches and roots, all the trees and plants, heaven and earth, seas and oceans, in fact, all things. For the Torah is the Name of the Holy One of Being. As the Name of the Holy One is engraved in the Ten Words (creative utterances) of Creation, so is the whole Torah engraved in the Ten Words (Decalogue), and these Ten Words are the Name of the Holy One, and the whole Torah is thus one Name, the Holy Name of God.

The whole Torah
The Zohar (Soncino Press), 3:278.

JOINING the FIRST with the LAST

Not only are all ten utterances at Sinai contained within the first word, they are all of one piece: one organic unity. The first utterance contains the germ of all that is yet to follow, just as the final utterance is the fruition of all that has come before. The first commences with the "I am" of God, and the last concludes with the "thou" of "your neighbor." Taken together the ten utterances are prototype and symbol for the entire revelation understood to be one long name of God.

To explain just how the first contains the last or how the last presumes the first is not so easy. "I am the Lord your God" somehow should contain "You shall not covet anything that belongs to your neighbor." And "You shall not covet anything that belongs to your neighbor" somehow should presume that "I am the Lord your God." The first and the last are, upon closer observation, probably the strangest of all the commandments. The first (according to Jewish tradition is "I am the Lord your God who brought you out of the land of Egypt, out of the house of bondage") is not even a commandment at all. It is only a statement. And statements cannot be followed or enforced. The last ("You shall not covet") is equally problematic since its observance or violation cannot

be publicly verified. Or if, as many believe, the first is a command to believe, then both the first and the last are requests
for an interior mental state. But interior mental states, like
thought crimes, are probably involuntary and therefore do
not carry any sense of culpability. You cannot help what
you believe or what you want. You simply believe what you
believe and want what you want. Nevertheless, through joining the first and most important utterance with the last and
most frequently violated commandment, the organic unity of
the entire revelation, can be resolved.

I AM and DO NOT COVET

As the first utterance begins with "I," so the last commandment concludes with "your neighbor," thereby com-
pleting the spectrum from me to you, one to another, I to
thou. By the time the echo of that first, almost soundless
aleph has reached the last commandment, "Do not covet,"
it seems to have lost most of its power. Not only is wanting
what other people have unpreventable, it is virtually universal. How trivial this prohibition against coveting when set
next to the Name of the Self of the Universe. Nevertheless,
according to at least Rabbi Yakum, "One who violates the
tenth commandment violates them all," even the first!

Violates them all
Midrash
Pesikta Rabbati
21.17.

The first utterance and the last commandment may be
joined to one another because they are simply different sides
of the same truth. They are each the cause of the other. Something like this is suggested by Rabbi Michal of Zolotchov, who
intuits that "not to covet" is not a commandment but a reward.

You shall not covet your neighbor's house ... or anything that is your neighbor's. How is it possible to
command someone concerning a mental state which

has no external manifestations? The answer is that this final utterance of the decalogue, "You shall not covet," is not so much a command as the Divine assurance of a reward. If a person is worthy (and fulfills) all the preceding nine utterances, God promises us that we will not covet anything that is our neighbor's—which is to say that your heart will be complete and you will rejoice in your allotted portion and with whatever you possess.

Your allotted portion
Mordecai HaKohen, *Al HaTorah: Selected Sayings on the Weekly Torah Portion* (Jerusalem, 1968), 218.

This is easy to understand if we take the first and the last utterance in their converse formulation. The first obviously changes from "I am the Lord your God" to "There are no others." And the tenth changes from "Do not want what belongs to your neighbor" to simply "Be content with what you have" and therefore with who you are.

If you are content with your portion, you will want nothing and you will lack nothing. You will be like the One who spoke "I am." It does not mean that you will not, nor ought not, change and grow; it means only that at this moment, in this place, you are all that you can be. No more, no less. You simply will be present in this *makom*, place, and by so being resemble the One who is also called *makom*, place. It is almost a tautology. Right now we can only be who we are. We are simply all that we can be. And once we recognize this, we can no longer covet anything because at this moment there is nothing else that we could possibly be. And if that is so, when we say "I am, *Anochi*, אנכי" we come very close to the One who spoke the first "I am." Through fulfilling the prohibition against coveting, we have at the same time "heard" the first utterance in a new way. To utter the "I am" is to want nothing else and, strange though it sounds, to want nothing else is the necessary prerequisite for all

[142]

genuine growth. The last commandment then is another way of saying the first utterance and together they are the touchstone for all spiritual growth. Growth must begin with self-acceptance; change begins with not trying to change.

SELF-ACCEPTANCE and CHANGE

You cannot become someone other than who you are until you know who you are. And you cannot know who you are until you accept who you are right now and in this place. For the time is now, not some other time; and the place is here, not somewhere else. And you are who you are, not anyone else.

A feature common to most neuroses, psychodynamic constellations opposed to change, is that they consume you with attempts to deny or escape their power, to try to act like they are not there. And yet it is precisely what you imagine you must do to escape their power that constitutes their chief symptomatology. What you consciously do to conceal, deny, and struggle against what you (unconsciously) fear you are, are the symptoms of your neurosis.

And liberation from their bondage comes from acceptance of how we behave and of who we are. "I am the Lord your God, who brought you out of the Land of Egypt, out of the house of bondage," can also be read, from "the Lord" through "house of bondage" as one long name of God. This is a God who is, above all, a God of freedom. God's Name is "the One who carries slaves to freedom." The slaves who were freed from Egypt were not freed until they could acknowledge and understand their own participation in their slavery. It takes more than a master to make a slave. A slave is someone who allows someone or something else to define him or herself. Not until we recognize our bondage can we begin to move toward freedom.

It is a paradox. Change begins not by trying to change. And what you imagine you must do in order to change yourself is often the very force that keeps you precisely the way you are. How else can you explain the years and decades of your own foiled plans for growth and broken resolutions. Consumed by an apparent passion to be "other" than who you are, you try to be who you are not, but in so doing succeed only in being a person who is trying to be other than who you are. Thus the goal of all therapy is self-discovery—the discovery not of another self but of one's true self. Beneath all the layers of wanting to be different, self-dissatisfaction, pretense, charade, and denial is a self. This self is a living dynamic force within everyone. And if you could remain still long enough here, now, in this very place, you would discover who you are. And by discovering who you are, you would at last be free to discover who you yet also might be.

You can be who you are, or you can pretend to be who you are not. If you choose the latter (as most of us have done since adolescence), an infinite variety of self-deceptions lie before you. You can pretend to be wise when you are ignorant, weak when you are strong, courageous when you are timid, confident when you are unsure. There is no end to the list. But remember this: none of these pretensions, no matter how noble, appropriate, or convincing, will fashion genuine change. They will instead require increasingly greater amounts of energy and enmesh you in increasingly complicated nets of deception. Or you can cease pretending to be someone you are not and discover at this moment who you are. Who am I writing these words? Who are you reading them? We are, in the imagery of the first utterance, selves

[144]

who are unable to hear the "I am, *Anochi*, אנכי" and there-fore unable to say it. Or in the language of the final com-mandment, we are selves largely defined by whom and what we covet. And real growth can happen only through heeding the first utterance and the last commandment.

God's "I am" has the psychotheological force not of dis-solving individual selves but of reminding us that we never were independent in the first place. Of course we are dis-crete individuals who move in different directions, but taken together we are each mirrors on some gently rotating mobile, or crystal prisms on some grand chandelier. We imagine that they can each say "I" and do so until they hear the Self of the Universe say that first almost soundless *alef* that means "I am," and then, for only a moment, they realize that their "selfhood," their "I," endures by virtue of its participation in some greater Self, some greater "I." In this way and from that time on, as long as the echo survives, they say "I" with a great reverence. Their selves are part of a greater Self.

The layers of pretense and self-delusion fall away, leav-ing now instead the innermost essence that knows its origin and destiny. This at last is a self that knows its place among other selves, perhaps not "I am" but "i am." This "i" is the dynamic force behind personal change. Who are we? Really? Not the public personae, nor the images, nor the professions, nor the apologies. Not the past, for that can only produce pride or guilt. Not the future, for that can only produce hope or fear. The first utterance is in the present. All that is said is the personal pronoun in the first person Singular form: "*Anochi*, אנכי, I."

The prohibition against coveting produces the same effect. If we are forbidden even to want anything belonging to someone else, we are left with only what is already ours. Do not covet her spouse or her house or her servants. Do not wish for his talent or his status or his style. Do not envy his past or her future. Instead accept your own. Not with stoic resignation but with quiet dignity.

At this moment (at least) things could be no other way. Only once you are able to know this will you again understand (hear) the "I am" that begins (and perhaps concludes) every revelation.

MY CARD

The first utterance is only God's self-announcement. God, as it were, says, "My card." There in the center is the Name of God. Then beneath it, in italics, "Frees Slaves." And in fine print, in the lower right-hand corner "Call any time."

HEART HARDENING

I used to be puzzled by why there were ten plagues. If God can split the sea, then surely God can free the children of Israel with a snap of the (divine) fingers. Furthermore, why would God harden Pharaoh's heart and thereby deprive him of any moral culpability for his obduracy? The answer, I am convinced, has more to do with the Jews than with Pharaoh and the Egyptians. Remember that while the Jews complained about their slavery, they also were distrustful of Moses and fearful of rising up. Indeed, before the first plague their hearts were frozen hard by the bitterness of their slavery.

Each successive plague seems to have an incremental effect on Pharaoh and on the children of Israel. One heart they harden, the other hearts they lighten with hope. For the Jews the effect will be that even contemplating serving God frees your heart. For Pharaoh the inescapable conclusion will be that enslaving others, serving yourself, and calling yourself a god gradually seals you off from life until your heart turns to stone that sinks in the sea.

The rate at which Pharaoh's heart becomes sclerotic is precisely the rate at which Israel's heart begins to lighten. Pharaoh does not lose his freedom, he merely lives out the consequences of his own arrogance and ambition.

This is the lesson: You refuse to know of anything sacred beyond yourself, you call yourself a god—go ahead, but it will turn your heart into a brick. And this is the other lesson: If you are willing to consider that your present slavery is of your own choice and that there is a Holy One beyond yourself who wants only that you be free to "serve in the wilderness," then your heavy heart can soar like a bird on eagle's wings.

HEARING the SELF of SINAI

I'll tell you what happened to Moses on Sinai. There was nothing audible, except his own breathing. Nothing visible that a video camera would pick up. And nothing different, except a new and strangely powerful sense of who he was. Now, for the first time, he knew that he was a discrete and autonomous human being. He knew furthermore that this sense—which later generations would call a self—was somehow mysteriously the result of and therefore eternally connected to some greater Self.

So many years earlier as a young shepherd he had sensed this but did not know what to call it. All he knew then, as he watched a bush burn (for what seemed like an eternity), was that somehow he himself also could be on fire and not be consumed. And now, on top of the same mountain, here it was again, the same sensation, only this time clear and unmistakable.

Now the first person singular pronoun, "*Anochi*, אנכי, I," meant something new and unimaginable. His sister had told him, when he was a little boy, that it was simply called the *aleph* of Creation, the first letter that was the mother of all articulate speech. But here hidden, trembling behind the rocks, he understood that this *aleph* was also the first letter not only for the Holy One of all Being, but also the name by which every person addresses his or her own self: "I." The first letter of the Hebrew alphabet, א, *Aleph*, and the letter that began God's invisible speech at Sinai, is also the first letter of the Hebrew word, "*Anochi*, אנכי, I."

For this reason, Sinai occurs whenever we reexperience that first barely audible letter that begins the name of *Anochi*, אנכי, "I," the Self. Whenever, in other words, like Moses, we are quiet long enough to become aware of the barely audible sound of our own breathing.

The VOICE UTTERING ITSELF

There is a fascinating irregularity in Numbers 7:89. After all the princes of Israel have brought their gifts of consecration, Moses is left alone in the newly completed wilderness tabernacle. The text reads: "[Moses] heard the Divine Voice speaking to him...." Given the context, that does not seem especially noteworthy. A very close reading however turns

All articulate speech Scholem, *On the Kabbalah*, 30–31.

Fascinating irregularity I am grateful to Rabbi Dr. Jonathan Magonet, principal of London's Leo Baeck Rabbinical College, who first called my attention to this anomaly.

up one extraneous dot, or vowel. Normally the Hebrew for "speaking, *midabbaer*" appears in the *piel* conjugation that places a dot, or *dagesh*, in the middle letter of the verbal root. But curiously here, in addition to the one in the *beit*, the *dalet* is also vocalized with a *dagesh* of its own. And if the conjugation is *piel*, that dot is not supposed to be there.

At times like this we are especially grateful for Rashi's commentary. Rashi too has noticed the irregularity and offers the explanation that our verb, *midabbaer*, is actually an odd form of what used to be *mitdabaer*, a *hitpael* conjugation with a letter *tav* that has been assimilated into the *dalet*. But now all that remains of the *tav* is the *dagesh* or dot. And all this renders the verse not "[Moses] heard the Divine Voice speaking to him," but, since the *hitpael* conjugation is reflexive, "[Moses] heard the Voice uttering itself." (I imagine in much the same way that ordinary folks looking into a mirror when no one is around, or at a starry night sky, or perhaps standing on the shore of the ocean wonder, "Who am I? What does it mean to have a self?")

But, of course, this only raises the deeper question: If the Divine Self is uttering itself and the Divine Self is also the source of your self, who then is listening? Or, when I wonder who "I" truly am, am I really alone or is another One present also?

The GREAT SELF

God is our sense of self, our innermost essence, encountered throughout all creation. Our selves are made of God's Self. But this does not mean that the world is our creation, or that we are God. It does mean that this awareness, this sense of uniqueness we feel cannot possibly have come just from ourselves. It is bigger than us and must be in every-one else. In all living things. In stones and water and fire. Everywhere. Indeed, this sense of self, this *Anochi*, אנכי, is so holy we correctly intuit that it has created us. We live and breathe through its radiance and compassion. It is the source of our vital energy. We are fulfilled through its service. And we secretly suspect that through making this one Self a conscious reality, history will at last be resolved into one C-major chord, the entire Torah pronounceable as one long, uninterrupted Name of God.

SELF-AWARENESS

Self is an orchestration of our awareness, an integration of consciousness holding everything together, making us whole and able to be called by a single name—our name. Self integrates and unifies our physical body, our thoughts, our actions. And it is the same with God and creation.

The universe too has a name by which it means to inte-grate its myriad contradictions into one organism. The uni-verse, like you and me, has a Self, a Self that nourishes and sustains each individual self. God is to being as the self is to us. God is the *Anochi*, אנכי, *shel Olam*, the "I" of the world, the Self of the Universe.

In the words of the philosopher and physician Moses Maimonides writing in the twelfth century, not only is God "the one who knows and that which is known; God is also … the knowing itself."

The knowing itself
Moses Maimonides, *Mishneh Torah*, *Hilkot Yesoday Torah*, 2.10.

Or, as Nachman of Bratslav observed:

The essence of a person is consciousness and there-fore wherever one is conscious, there is the whole person. And likewise one who knows and attains an understanding of God is actually in God. The greater a person's knowing, the more that person is included in the root, in God.

One of my high school students once asked me if I could prove there was a God. Instead I asked her if she had a self. She thought for a moment and said, "Of course."

"And is your self important to you?"
"Very," she replied.
"And where would you be," I pushed, "without your self?"
"In big trouble."
"Can you prove you have one?"
She smiled. "I get what you mean."

SPIRITUALITY

The essence of spirituality is a return to the self, a redirection of vision of the one who asks the question, an almost serendipitous discovery that what is sought is, and has always been, right here all along. "It," in other words, is never somewhere else. Could this stubborn insistence that God has no body whatsoever be another way of keeping this primary and holy truth alive? If God has no body, then God is nowhere. And I need go nowhere.

Indeed, as Alexander Altmann observed:

... Finding God and worshiping God is but another way of saying that we have found our self. For every act of submission to God unifies our being and means a birth, as Rabbi Nachman of Bratslav tells us. Thus

Included in the root
Nachman of Bratslav, *Likkutei Moharan* 21:11. I am grateful to Arthur Green for calling this to my attention.

people are spiritually reborn in God, and God is, as it were, reborn in people.

Reborn in people
Altmann, "God and the Self," 146.

Spirituality is always in reference to two "I"s, two selves. The "i" of the person and the "I" of the Universe. It is religion in a personal mode, religion from the point of view of the "i" of yourself and from the point of view of the "I" of the Universe. Spirituality is not about someone else or even about yourself in some cool, self-reflective, objective manner; nor is it about the past or the future. It is personal and immediate. Spirituality is the presence of God. And only rarely—once in a generation or even less—is the presence of God accompanied by a heavenly chorus or light beaming out of the recipient's facial apertures. Most of the time that presence is very quiet, so quiet it can be drowned out by the slightest noise or lost to the slightest distraction. Indeed, God's presence already permeates all creation. We name it when we are born with our first cry and whisper it as we die with our last breath. It wants only to be made tangible through our hands.

We are agents, instruments of God's presence. We are not at odds with the Self of the Universe; we are part of it. And to be aware of this is to give our lives ultimate meaning and purpose. To realize that we are servants, through everything that we do, with or without our consent, is to be able to do anything; it is our empowerment and fulfillment. Spirituality is a dimension of living where we are aware of God's presence. It is being concerned with how what we do affects God and how what God does affects us.

What we do affects God
I am grateful to Martin Strelser for this insight.

TEA with LEMON

After my father (his memory is a blessing) had his first big heart attack we gathered daily around his hospital bed. We knew he was recovering when he began to complain about the hospital food service. One evening he was especially frustrated that he could not seem to get anyone to bring him a cup of tea with lemon. First the nurse was busy. Then he got tea but no lemon. By the time the lemon arrived, the hot water had grown cold. They took away the tray and brought him another cup of tea, but there was no lemon! I could see the disappointment in his face. Then it hit me. "Wait just two minutes, Dad. I'll be right back." I ran down five flights of stairs (the hospital elevators would have taken forever), through the cafeteria line and grabbed a handful of lemons, back up the stairs to his room. "Here," I said. He smiled and drank the tea with lemon. There was even some left for me. What a sacred joy to do something for someone you love.

UNIO MYSTICA

"If mysticism is the quintessence of religion," then, as Moshe Idel opines, "the quintessence of mysticism is the sense of union with God."

Idel's book is a watershed. It overturns much of Gershom Scholem, who, in retrospect, now clearly seems to have had a blind spot when it came to imagining Jews becoming one with God. Scholem was such an extraordinary intellect that people never thought to question him. But Moshe Idel meticulously demonstrates the master's bias and how Jews, throughout the ages, like the pious of every other spiritual tradition, have sought the experience of unity with God, or *devekut*, (which literally means "cleaving") and succeeded.

The classic sources for *devekut* are: Deuteronomy 4:4, "But you that *cleave* unto the Lord, your God this day are alive every one of you this day" and Isaiah 43:11, "I, I am

Quintessence of mysticism
Moshe Idel, *Kabbalah: New Perspectives* (New Haven: Yale University Press, 1988), 35.

Sources for *devekut*
Moshe Idel, *Studies in Ecstatic Kabbalah* (Albany: State University of New York Press, 1988), 11–12. It seems that the phrase "I, I" is an exclamation by a mystic, indicating awareness of becoming divine.

the Lord." The repetition of *Anochi*, אנכי, in the latter passage is taken to mean that the first "I" is God and the second is the self. As Idel observes, "the worshiper is no longer himself or herself, for the worshiper is fully absorbed, in that moment, in the Nothingness of divinity.

Nothingness of divinity
Green and Holtz, *Your Word Is Fire*, 14–15.

The MODES of DEVEKUT

Three forms of *devekut*
Idel, *Kabbalah*, 39ff.

Idel identifies three forms of *devekut* that precisely correspond to what I have long suspected were the three kinds of religious personalities. In other words, first comes personality, then theology. Idel begins with what he calls Aristotelian *devekut*. I would call it cognitive *devekut*. In this form of union, during the act of cognition the knower and the known become one. This is a description of the experience of the loss of self by a personality who is cerebral, rational, linear, left-brain dominant. Someone we today might call a head person.

Supernal form of God
Talmud tractate *Berakhot* 6a: "What is written in God's *tefillin*? 'Who is like your people Israel, one nation on the earth.'... The Holy One said to Israel: You have made Me a unique entity in the world [by reciting the *shema*] ... and I shall make you a unique entity in the world [with the words in My *tefillin*." *Itturay Torah*, 1:126.

A second mode of *devekut* is the *devekut* of behavior. In this experience, one seeks to literally affect and, as it were, to help God through specific actions. It is predicated on the similarity and interdependence of the human body with the supernal form of God. In this mode of *devekut*, one's will and actions become God's. If one becomes a servant of God, then his or her deed is also God's action. By repairing things here, we repair them above. A personality drawn to such cleaving to God is action-oriented, a doer, an achiever, a fixer, someone who wants to repair the world. If the first personality was a head person, the second would be a hands person.

The third form of *devekut* is the *devekut* of prayer. Concerned with reuniting the soul with its root, the focus of this third personality is neither cerebral nor behavioral but emotional. Such a soul is drawn to closing his eyes, losing herself in song, sitting in silence. I would call such a one a heart person. And thus for each type of religious personality (or different aspects of the same person) becoming one with God finds its unique expression.

We don't want just to read about what God wants. We don't want someone else telling us what God wants either. We don't even want God telling us what God wants. We want our eyes to be God's eyes so that we can see the world the way God sees it. We want our teaching to be God's Torah. We want our hands to do God's work. We want our prayers to be God's prayers. We want to want what God wants. *Devekut*: being one with God. At last the "little i, Anochi, אנכי" and the "Great I, Anochi, אנכי, of All creation" are one.

The ONE WHO ASKS IS the ONE WHO HEARS

I am now convinced that *devekut* is more than being one with God. *Devekut* is a theological metaphor for stopping the inner conversation we routinely carry on inside our head between the disparate parts of our psyche. *Devekut* is a metaphor for self-unification. *Devekut* is a time when the outer person is revealed to be illusory, a figment of language, an iron barrier separating us from God. Now only an un-self-conscious awareness remains, an awareness that bears a wonderful similarity to the divine. A woman in my congregation on Yom Kippur once offered a personal prayer in which she prayed for the wisdom to "wish to be who she was."

Devekut is when the one who asks and the one who hears are the same. We realize to our embarrassment that we have been who we were all along and only linguistic convention tricked us into thinking that we were someone else. We cannot make God do what we want, but in thinking, doing, and praying what God wants, we become one with God and ourselves.

The OWNER of the WORDS

"Can I ask you a personal question?" ventured Jacob.

"Of course," de León nodded.

"Who really wrote the *Zohar*? I mean, was it really Shimon bar Yohai, or did you forge the whole thing?"

"The honest truth," replied de León, "is that I don't know. I could say either 'yes' or 'no.'"

"C'mon. What kind of answer is that?"

"Look, I won't lie to you. My hand wrote the words of the *Zohar*. There is no question about that. But they are *not my words*. Someone else wrote them. When I sat down to write, it was as if some other soul were in command of my body. I don't remember writing any of it. I look now at the pages and read them for the first time. I swear to you: not one word of the *Zohar* is mine."

"Then whose are they?"

"If I had to guess, I'd say Shimon bar Yohai's."

אכן יש ה' במקום הזה ואנכי לא ידעתי

I didn't know that my name was part of God's Name

7 / OSTROPOL

SELF

1648 was a bad year to be a Jew in Poland. This was the year the Messiah was supposed to come. Instead, a Ukrainian patriot Bogdan Khelmnitsky massacred some 100,000 unarmed Jews. Today in Moscow, a major boulevard honors his name. It is just down the street from what was until just recently the city's only remaining synagogue.

One of the people Khelmnitsky's Cossack army killed was Shimshon ben Pesach Ostropoler. On July 22, in the town of

Shimson ben Pesach Ostropoler Ostropol, Ukraine, d. 1648.

[159]

Polonoye, Poland
Today Polonoye is in Ukraine.

Refuge in the synagogue
Encyclopedia Judaica, s. v. "Polonnoye."

Kabbalistic demonology
Scholem, *Kabbalah*, 325.

Polonoye, Poland, Shimshon sought refuge in the synagogue with 300 Jews of his community. (They wrapped themselves in their prayer shawls.) Rabbi Shimshon ben Pesach was the community's preacher and *maggid*, or storyteller, and was regarded as one of the greatest Polish scholars of Lurianic Kabbalah. Gershom Scholem considers Rabbi Ostropoler's *Sefer Karnayim* to be the last original text in Kabbalistic demonology. He was a mystic who gave previously unknown names to the *kelipot*, "the broken shards of creation." No trace has been found yet of his major work, a commentary on the *Zohar* titled *Machaneh Dan*. We know virtually nothing of his personal life.

Rabbi Shimshon had been hoping to meet Jacob for some time now and may have been even mildly frustrated that the encounter had taken so long. You know how it is. If you study a text long enough, the characters on the pages come to life and speak lines only you can hear. And the biblical text is no ordinary text. Not only do the words live in us, but we live in them. From time to time, after serious study, we are surprised, inspired, and humbled to find ourselves as last-minute additions in the spaces between words or even stand-ins for its characters, animals, and inanimate objects. In any case, Shimshon may be the one who finally understood what Jacob discovered about God.

JACOB SLEPT on MORIAH

Midrashic tradition, like other primary process modes of thinking, ignores the assumptions of calendars and maps. Times and places customarily separated by centuries and continents appear side by side without embarrassment; sometimes they are even fused. Ordinary boundaries dissolve during this search for deeper meaning.

The Midrash, for instance, records Rabbi Juda bar Seemon's teaching that Jacob's ladder actually stood on the site of the Temple Mount in Jerusalem, while its top arched over Beth El where Jacob slept. Since the place of Jacob's dream, somewhere in the Judean desert, and the site of the Temple Mount in Jerusalem were both places where direct access to God was experienced (according to primary process logic), they must be related, connected.

Where Jacob slept Midrash *Genesis Rabba* 69.17.

Another midrash goes further. Here Beth El, where Jacob slept, and Mount Moriah, where Abraham bound Isaac on the altar, become the same. Playing on the similar sound, first of Jacob's words, "How awesome (Hebrew, *Norah*) is this place," and then on the name of the site where Isaac was bound, "Moriah" (also from the Hebrew root meaning "awesome"), the midrash concludes that Beth El and Moriah must be identical, "the place where religious awe entered the world."

Awesome is this place Genesis 28:17.

Where religious awe entered Midrash *Genesis Rabba* 55.7.

Another constellation of legends further explains that Mount Moriah, the site of the Temple itself, was uprooted and came to Jacob when he dreamed the ladder. So now the dreamscape includes by implication all places where heaven meets earth, where life circles open and close. In the world of the spirit, they are identical. Wherever holiness is awakened, wherever the beginning of a circle meets its end, wherever God appears, a ladder of light is erected that reaches heaven.

Constellation of legends Talmud tractate *Hullin* 91b.

Site of the Temple itself Rashi; *Itturay Torah*, 2:248.

Two decades later Jacob will return to this same place and have his second great spiritual encounter. No longer a young cheat on the run, this time he will be a man with two wives, two concubines, eleven sons, at least one daughter, and great wealth. But they will be no protection from his past; he must go alone. He will send them all across the ford at the river Jabok and remain by himself. There he will

This same place Genesis 32:23ff.

Bless him
with the name
Rabbi Dr.
Jonathan
Magonet,
principal of
the Leo Baeck
College in
London, has
suggested
that perhaps
Jacob was
hoping again
for another
"ladder dream"
of reassurance.

wrestle with one whose name he will never know, yet one who will bless him with the name of Israel.

In the Talmud we slide between the dream of the ladder and the night wrestler without any acknowledgment that an entire generation has passed. The encounters occur simultaneously. Perhaps the rabbis of the Midrash knew something about the nature of the religious experiences on Moriah and at Beth El that survives only in these fantasies.

Slide between
the dream
Talmud tractate
Hullin 91a–b.

Perhaps if Jacob will not return to Moriah to "complete the family's spiritual business," revisit the place where his grandfather almost killed his father, then Mount Moriah will come to him. Alone at night while he sleeps they assemble: a ladder, an unnamed wrestler, a mountain, his grandfather Abraham, his great-grandfather Terah who worshiped idols. Now Jacob will close the circle, take his place in line. God, what a night!

Last of
ten trials
Ginzberg,
Legends, 1:217,
5:218 n. 52.

GREAT-GRANDPA WORSHIPED IDOLS

Leave his
father's house
Lewis M.
Barth, "Lection
for the Second
Day of Rosh
Hashanah:
A Homily
Containing
the Legend of
the Ten Trials
of Abraham,"
*Hebrew Union
College Annual*
58 (1988)
(Hebrew);
Ginzberg,
Legends,
1:217–18.

The temple will be erected in the same place, not only where Jacob dreamed (and wrestled?) but where his grandfather Abraham nearly killed his father Isaac. There are reasons why he must return to this place. Here is where the older generation tries to convince the younger about the meaning of life. Even though the attempt is doomed from the start, somehow, in the failing, both generations learn about God.

According to rabbinic legend, Abraham's test that he sacrifice his son, was already the last of ten trials. The first occurred back in his own Babylonian boyhood when God told him to leave his father's house. I can't get it out of my head that the key to decoding the binding of Isaac legend, or, as it is known in Hebrew, the *Akedah*, is concealed back in the strange relationship Abraham, our father, had with Terah, his father. I am chastened to learn over and over again that patterns in a family recur from one generation to the next. Abraham violently separates from his father, almost murders his son. So it goes.

In his poem, "God of Abraham, God of Isaac," Joel Rosenberg has Isaac say after the *Akedah*: "(His voice now changed into a man's): 'But tell me, *Abba* [Daddy], you have left your father's house. And will I do the same, and will my child?'" Perhaps in order for one generation to yield to another requires children to smash their parents' idols, and parents to nearly kill their progeny. Perhaps this is what the Midrash means when it speaks of these events as the first and the last of the ten trials Abraham had to endure.

And will my child?
Joel Rosenberg, "God of Abraham, God of Isaac," *National Jewish Monthly* 90, no. 8 (April 1976).

According to the Midrash, Terah ran an idol boutique in the Land of Ur. One day, it seems, the old man had to go out of town on a business trip and asked his son to mind the store. When Abraham was alone, he took a hatchet and (in what can only be called a fit of adolescent, iconoclastic rage) smashed all his father's gods, except the biggest one, into whose hands he mischievously placed the hatchet. When Terah returned he cried, "What happened?"

"I cooked a delicious dinner for them," replied his son, "but they all fought for the food. Then that big one over there took the hatchet and smashed the others. See, it's still in his hand!"

The old man was enraged. "Why they're just dumb statues of wood and stone! I made them all myself!"

"So how come you pray to them, you moron?" Abe grabbed the hatchet, shattered the last idol, and fled.

Grabbed the hatchet
Ginzberg, Legends, 1:214–15.

The OLD HOUSE

What I wonder is, did they ever see each other after the split? How did Terah feel. Did he pick up the hatchet and shout, "You better run or I'll use this on you!" Or did he just sit on his heap of smashed idols and cry. Did they ever talk to one another again? Maybe once a year, after the *Akedah* was read in the synagogue on *Rosh Hashanah*, a three-minute phone call? If they didn't speak, did Abe ever think about his father back there in the old house? Did Abe return home to visit his father in the hospital? Were they ever reconciled? And I wonder if Jewish neurosis down to this day might not be the result of the violent way in which Abraham seems to have separated from his father and all his father's gods or if, on the other hand, that is the source of whatever unique insight Jews possess into the human condition. From one generation to another, for all these centuries. Who can tell? And whatever became of Terah?

Phrase in Genesis
Genesis 15:15.

Fathers in peace
Itturay Torah, 1:111.

Child confers privileges
Talmud tractate *Sanhedrin* 104a.

Rabbi Yehudah Leib Eger of Lublin, writing in the middle of the nineteenth century, is fascinated by the phrase in Genesis where Abraham is assured that he will go to his "fathers in peace." Rashi also asks, could Abraham join his father, Terah, who worshiped idols, in paradise? One possible explanation comes from the Talmud, which reads that "a child confers privileges on a parent." Perhaps Terah was permitted entrance on account of Abraham, his son. But this only raises another problem, notes Eger, because the verse also says "fathers" in the plural, implying that not only Terah would be in paradise, but also Nahor, Terah's father, as well. But by what merit could Nahor, whose son was an idolator, possibly have earned paradise? We can only conclude that Terah must have made *teshuva*, repentance, and that, since "a son confers privileges on his father," Terah must have also earned a place for Nahor, his own father, to be with him in Eden.

Rabbinic authorities disagree over how old Isaac was at the time of the *Akedah*. The story evokes an adolescent: strong enough to carry the wood, yet young enough to want to please his father. Others have suggested Isaac was much older. A full-grown man, thirty-seven years old, on the other side of a midlife crisis, who knew all along what was going on and how to play his part in the drama. According to one midrash:

> While Abraham was building the altar, Isaac kept handing him the wood and the stones. Abraham was like a man who builds the wedding house for his son, and Isaac was like a man getting ready for the wedding feast, which he does with joy.

One curious feature of the *Akedah* is a frequently noted omission. In a tale that obviously has been crafted with great precision, how odd that, on two separate occasions, on their way *to* the mountain, we are told that Abraham and Isaac "went along, both of them together," yet after whatever it was that really happened up there, we read only "and Abraham returned to his servants." What happened to Isaac? What did the father and the son talk about as they went along, both of them together? "Tell me about grandpa Terah again, Dad, and how you used to work in his shop when you were a kid. Did you really smash all his statues?"

Often sacred legends can be decoded by broadening our definition of participating characters. Perhaps it is time to

Thirty-seven years old
Midrash *Genesis Rabba* 56.8.

Ready for the wedding
Midrash *WaYosha*, 73; Shalom Spiegel, *The Last Trial: On the Legends and Lore of the Command to Abraham to Offer Isaac as a Sacrifice—The Akedah*, trans. Judah Goldin (New York: Schocken, 1967), 135.

Both of them together
Genesis 22:6, 8.

Abraham returned
Genesis 22:19.

The form
of a bull
Nahum
M. Sarna,
*Exploring
Exodus: The
Heritage of
Biblical Israel*
(New York:
Schocken,
1987), 218.

reconsider the ram as a more important player in the drama. Perhaps it was more than a surrogate sacrifice. As Nahum Sarna observes, "The depiction of a god in the form of a bull was widespread throughout the entire ancient Near East. That animal was a symbol of lordship, strength, vital energy, and fertility, and was either deified and made an object of worship or, on account of these sovereign attributes, was employed in representation of deity." We remember also that the Baal idol the Hebrew prophets railed against was a bull. Furthermore the sin of the Northern Kingdom of Israel was the worship of a cow. Indeed, the paradigmatic idol in Jewish tradition is a golden calf. Perhaps it was no accident that a ram was slaughtered.

Perhaps it was not Abraham who killed the ram after all. Perhaps Isaac did the slaughtering because he realized that after all those years even Abraham's new unitary god had begun to harden into a graven and predictable image. No longer the unrepresentable fire of Being but now the culturally convenient image of a ram. "This is my God, O Isaac, who brought me out of Ur of the Chaldeans...." Who can say? Only the two of them were up there together. And Isaac did not return.

Isaac was
thirty-five
*Tanna Debe
Eliyyahu:
The Lore of
the School of
Elijah*, trans.
William
Braude and
Israel Kapstein
(Philadelphia:
Jewish Publica-
tion Society,
1981), 103,
105; Ginzberg,
Legends, 1:206.

From another midrash comes what may be the missing piece. Apparently, Abraham's father did not die of a broken heart, never to be heard from again. We read that "for many years Terah continued to be a witness to his son's glory, God accepted his repentance and when he died he was admitted into paradise. Indeed, one tradition teaches that he did not die until Isaac was thirty-five years old." Which, as we have already noted, may have been about the same time that Abraham and Isaac went up on Mount Moriah. The old man was waiting for his son, Abraham, when he came down the mountain alone. He looked into Abraham's eyes freshly washed with tears and saw that they were now clear and bright.

"Dad? Is that you? What are you doing here? I thought you were dead. How did you get here? Isaac, my son is gone. I'm so confused. Is Mom still alive? God told me to take Isaac up there and kill him on an altar. Isaac even carried the wood himself. Then I don't know what happened. I tried to show Isaac how this ram we found was a beautiful way to imagine God, but he only said I was blind. He said that my god had stopped moving years ago. He called me a moron. We fought. There was screaming and blood, then Isaac hacked off the ram's head. Look, I have one of its horns. Then I remembered what I had done to you. But when I turned around, Isaac was gone. Dad, I'm sorry. I didn't mean to destroy your idols. Did you really believe in them? Were they covered by the insurance? I mean, I didn't mean to hurt you; I just wanted to show you what I couldn't seem to tell you. Then I ran away and I was too ashamed to go back. All these years. And now my Isaac is gone. I don't know where he is. I swear I didn't kill him. See, I have this horn of the ram he killed instead. Oh Daddy, I love you. Forgive me.... Now I understand."

Terah was silent. He reached out his arms and held Abraham, his little boy. "And they went along, both of them together." And now Jacob was there too and saw the whole thing. As William Faulkner observed, "Not only is the past relevant, it's not even done!"

HANDS of GOD, EYES of FATHER

During the last decade of my father's life, his memory is a blessing, he combined his artistic dexterity and a life-long fascination with architecture to make hundreds of miniature buildings. Most widely known were a series of over fifty museum-quality synagogue models, but he also completed houses, barns, sheds, any building shape that caught his imagination.

Like any artist, he would often use "reality" as a jumping-off point, then give his imagination free reign. During my boyhood I never noticed his fascination with architectural structure as anything out of the ordinary. Like so many dimensions of one's parents, it was so ordinary that only in retrospect did this fascination emerge as one of the mysterious themes of his life. We would go on family driving vacations. He would point out an interesting farmhouse or stand so long gazing at a barn that I would ask him what he saw.

And in this way, his sensitivity became mine. Now he is gone and all I have are the models he built and the continuing enjoyment I derive from looking at the shapes of buildings. Only now, of course, there is always a tinge of sadness when I realize he will never be able to see this extraordinary house with such interesting gables and such a long shed porch.

Not long ago, while giving some lectures in a faraway city, my hosts lodged me at a nearby inn situated in the middle of a restored antique village. Like many, this suburban community had grown around an old town center the locals had been wise enough to preserve. There must have been a half-dozen blocks of picturesque shops and homes. I stopped in front of one after another, remembering my father, sad that we could not share the sight. And then it came to me. Since he no longer had physical eyes, I would have to look at each building with special care and twice as long, for from now on I would have to see the world for both of us.

Perhaps it is the same way with human beings and God. God's eyes are now our eyes. God's ears are now our ears. And God's hands are ours. It is up to us, what God will see and hear, up to us, what God will do. Look at the world, you are seeing with God's eyes. Look at your hands, they are the hands of God.

PACK of CIGARETTES

Jacob could remember how when he was younger, his father would tell him stories, stories about the God of Abraham and his chariot. Jacob and Isaac would walk, the two of them together, through the long violet shadows after supper. Sometimes they would walk down to the corner drugstore for a newspaper, or a candy bar, or a pack of cigarettes before Abraham quit smoking. But it was only an excuse for the two of them to walk together. Often they would walk a long way without even saying anything, Jacob feeling important that his father wanted to spend time with him and feeling dumb that he could not think of anything important to say. That is the way it is with fathers and sons. They shared the silence of a boy and a man, "being men" together. Sometimes the man would put his hand on the boy's shoulder.

The INVISIBLE CHARIOT

If you are a Jew and you have a mystical experience, Gershom Scholem once told me, you most likely will behold the *merkava*, Ezekiel's chariot. The job of a religious tradition is to give imagery, symbolism, and grammar to experiences that finally transcend all language. Christians will behold Christ on the cross; Mohammedans, the face of the Prophet; and Buddhists, the true Nothing; but Jews who behold the Holy One of Being see the *merkava*, the chariot, the paradigmatic image of the Jewish mystical experience.

Later in the tenth
Ezekiel 10:14.

In the first chapter of Ezekiel (and later in the tenth), a priest of the now-destroyed first temple in Jerusalem, exiled with his people to the strange and faraway land of Babylonia, has a psychedelic vision. Dangerous business this, trying to catch a glimpse of God. According to rabbinic tradition, of all topics only two—the *merkava* and *ma'asey bereshit*, the mystery of creation—are forbidden to be taught in the presence of more than three people. In other words, the chariot belongs in the same category as ultimate reality. And like creation (which may have a lot to do with sexuality and procreation), beholding God is intimate and dangerous.

Forbidden to be taught
Maimonides, *Mishneh Torah, Hilkot Yesoday Torah*, 4.10.

Ezekiel's words are clear enough, but the scene they evoke is confusing at best. A thunderhead in the distance and some kind of pulsating (electrical?) brightness. God's throne (no longer stationary in the Holy of Holies safe in the Jerusalem Temple) appears on a chariot. Is God seated on it, or is it empty? The chariot has four wheels. But each wheel is a living creature. And each creature has four faces: lion, eagle, ox, and human being. It is hardly surprising therefore to read in the *Zohar* that Jacob's dream also included a vision of the *merkava*, Ezekiel's chariot.

Ezekiel's chariot
Zohar I 150a.

Second chariot
Joseph Dan, "Origins of Jewish Mysticism," Hebrew Union College, Jerusalem, Mar. 11, 1988; Midrash *Exodus Rabba* 3.2.

One more detail is important: Chapter ten of Ezekiel is called the second chariot because there the *merkava* is described again in an almost identical way. But there is a subtle modification. The ox is gone. In its stead a cherub has been substituted. The Talmud opines that the ox was an embarrassment, just a bit too similar to the golden calf for comfort, and therefore it had to be replaced. Other scholars suggest that in the ancient world a cherub was not the cupid-like child of English mythology. For while it had wings and a human head, it also had the body of a bull or a calf. Indeed, in Near Eastern temples the throne was guarded by cherubim. Professor Hartum also has noted that the word for "ox" in Aramaic looks like cherub.

Ox was an embarrassment
Talmud tractate *Hagigah* 13b.

Looks like cherub
Ezekiel 10:14; A. Hartum, ed., *Sifrei HaMikra, Sefer Yekhezkiel* (Tel Aviv: Yavneh Publishing, 1972), note on the same verse.

The *DRIVER'S SEAT*

Maybe he had seen the chariot too often, maybe he had higher powers, but Ostropol every now and then knew too much. It was as if his frail body was not big enough to handle the powerful, occasional jolts of energy which flowed through him. Like a lightning rod, he trembled, he perspired, his face flushed, and his eyes seemed to go in and out of focus. He had broken through some kind of barrier that left him exposed to the elements and infinite meaning. He was able to discern significance in everything, not only in words and actions, but even in letters and silence. Meaning streamed through him from everything.

The contemporary talmudist and mystic Adin Steinsaltz wasn't intentionally speaking of Shimshon ben Pesach; nevertheless the description could easily fit:

At the highest level of holiness are those persons who have achieved a state in which their whole personalities and all of their actions are inseparably joined to the divine holiness. Of these persons it is said that they have become a 'chariot' [*merkava*] for the

[171]

shekhinah [the Divine Presence] and, like the chariot, they are totally yielded up to the One who sits on
the driver's seat, the throne of glory, and they consti-
tute a part of the throne of glory itself, even though
they are flesh and blood, human beings like all other
human beings.

**Flesh
and blood**
Adin Steinsaltz,
*The Thirteen
Petalled Rose,*
trans. Yehuda
Hanegbi
(New York:
Basic Books,
1980), 82.

The I, i DID NOT KNOW

The Ostropoler's insight assumes one of the primary
axioms of all Jewish spirituality. Since God revealed the
Torah, not only is what it says holy, ultimate truth but so is
each word and even each letter. Each can be a gateway, as
it were, into the divine psyche. Such logic initially strikes
the Western mind as contrived and self-serving. However, in
reality, this is no more artificial than handwriting analysis or
the meticulous scrutiny paid by many students of Freud to
everyday verbal mistakes or the devoted concentration we
all pay to letters written us by a distant lover. If one can gain
important insights into everyday matters by close attention
to detail, then how much the more can we learn if the subject
under discussion is none other than the ultimate source of
all meaning in the universe: the Torah.

The first word
Genesis 28:16.

Basing his interpretation on the *Zohar*'s idea that Jacob
beheld the *merkava*, the chariot, and that Jacob obviously
must have been cognizant that living creatures carry the
divine throne, Shimshon Ostropoler notices that the first
word that Jacob said when he awoke is an odd particle of
speech, אכן *awchayn*. Occurring only twice in the Torah,
awchayn is customarily rendered as "surely" or "indeed."
However, in our passage something like "Oh, my God!" or
even Simply "Wow!" better captures Jacob's exclamation.
You meet God, you say, "Wow!"

**Twice in
the Torah**
The other place
is in Exodus
2:14, where
Moses,
confronted by
a fellow
Israelite after
killing the
Egyptian
taskmaster,
says, "Surely
the matter is
known...."

Rabbi Shimshon is struck by the coincidence that the three Hebrew letters which spell אכן *awchayn*: א *aleph*, כ *chaf*, ן *nun* are also three of the four letters of אנכי *Anochi*, or, "I," spelled, א *aleph*, נ *nun*, כ *char*, and י *yod* later on in the verse.

Is it possible that the coincidence is not accidental but a deliberate hint at some deeper layer of meaning? Perhaps אכן *awchayn* and אנכי *Anochi* are related. Perhaps Jacob realized something about the relationship between the creatures who carry the chariot and his own self, his own "I." Perhaps Jacob saw something in the chariot that enabled him to realize he was mistaken about the number of creatures who carry the chariot.

Whereas אכן *awchayn* only has three letters, the word for "I," אנכי *Anochi*, has the same three and a fourth, a י *yod*. I had thought there were three, but now I realize that there are four. Until this moment I did not know about the fourth. (But we are already anticipating.)

"Tell me please," asked the Ostropoler, "who carries the chariot?"

"Three creatures," answers Jacob, his student, the third patriarch of the Jewish people.

"And why do you say three?"

"Because אכן *awchayn* is spelled with three letters. א *aleph* is the first letter of *aryeh* or lion. כ *chaf* is the first letter *keruv* or cherub. And ן *nun* is the first letter of *nesher* or eagle. *Awchayn* represents the three creatures: *aryeh, keruv, nesher,* lion, cherub, and eagle. And אכן *awchayn* is an acronym for them. They were in this place, and I, i didn't know."

"Good," says Ostropoler. "But there is still more. Do you remember how you learned from Dov Baer of Mezritch that there was an extra 'i' in the second half of what you said?

"God was here because I stopped being aware of my 'i.'"
Sure three creatures were there and you didn't know it, but
there was something else you didn't know either, something
about your own self. Look more closely at what you said."

"*Awchayn*: aleph, chaf, nun, lion, cherub, eagle were
here," Jacob rehearsed his insight, "and I, i didn't know."

"And how do you spell אנכי *Anochi*, the word for 'I'?"

"*Aleph, nun, chaf, yod.* Look at that. The word for 'I,'
אנכי *Anochi* has the same three letters as אכן *awchayn*, plus
an additional fourth one, י *yod.*

The FOURTH CREATURE

"*Aleph* is the first letter for lion. *Nun*, the first letter of
eagle. And *chaf* the first of cherub. Now if *Anochi* which has
four letters is also an acronym, of what word is *yod* the first
letter?" coaxed Rabbi Shimshon ben Pesach Ostropoler.

Being normal, Jacob (whose name in Hebrew is pronounced, *Yaakov*—first letter *yod*) naturally thought first of
himself, and, being normal, he also concealed his first guess
from the teacher, thinking he would be judged guilty of egotism. So instead he replied, "I don't know."

"What do you mean you don't know!" scowled Ostropoler. "Think. What did the fourth creature look like. Was it an
animal?"

Yaakov began to sweat. "It looked like a human being,
not bad looking. I suppose it looked a little like me."

One midrash:

The angels descending the ladder beheld Jacob's
sleeping face and exclaimed, "This is the face of one
of the four creatures who are carrying the chariot!"
At the same time, the angels on the earth ascending

[174]

the ladder did so to behold the face of Jacob on the chariot.

And another:

The Holy One of Being said to Jacob: "Jacob, you are very precious to me. For I have, as it were, set your image on My throne, and with your name the angels praise Me and say: 'Blessed be the Lord, the God of Israel [Jacob] for ever and ever.'"

"A little like you? How about exactly like you! You think I and all these other messengers going up and down the ladder are just some kind of religious parade for your evening entertainment. We are curious. We are amazed, just like you should be amazed."

"I don't believe it," said Jacob. "Not after what I've done to my father and my brother ..."

"Believe it," said the Ostropoler. "It's you up there and it's you down here. Precisely the same creature. The first letter of your name, ו *yod*, is the fourth and final letter of אנכי *Anochi*, 'I,' the last letter of God's name. You are an indispensable ingredient of God. You carry the chariot. You stop carrying it, it doesn't move. The correct reading of what you said is: 'Wow! God was in this place and I did not know it was i!'"

"The reason the self and God are mutually exclusive is that they are already made of the same stuff. God is in this place, here where you are, and the reason you do not realize it is because you are already busy, along with the lion, the eagle, and the cherub, carrying the chariot. Your self is an essential part of the Holy One (Himself, Herself), the Self. The first letter of your name is the final letter of the word for the Self of the Universe. The first letter of your name is the

The face of Jacob Midrash *Pirke deRabbi Eliezer*, ch. 35; Talmud tractate *Hullin* 91b; Midrash *Genesis Rabba* 68.12.

Your image on My throne Midrash *Numbers Rabba* 4.1. The forefathers themselves are the chariot. Midrash *Genesis Rabba* 82.6, 47.6.

Blessed be the Lord Psalm 41:14.

[175]

last letter of God's. Look at your hands. You are looking at the hands of God."

GOOD MORNING

And with that Rabbi Shimson ben Pesach Ostropoler turned and joined the others now departing this world and the dream, making their way back up the ladder until the occasions of their respective births would bring them back again.

> And [Jacob] was astonished, and he said, "This place is awesome. It must be the very Home of God, the very gateway to Heaven itself."

> Jacob got up early that morning. He took one of the stones he had used as a pillow and he set it up as a marker. Then he anointed it. And he called the name of that place, the Home of God.

The Home of God
Genesis 28:17–19.

אכן יש ה' במקום הזה ואנכי לא ידעתי

EPILOGUE

YOUR TORAH,
GOD'S TORAH

Each person has a Torah, unique to that person, his or her innermost teaching. Some seem to know their Torahs very early in life and speak and sing them in a myriad of ways. Others spend their whole lives stammering, shaping, and rehearsing them. Some are long, some short. Some are intricate and poetic, others are only a few words, and still others can only be spoken through gesture and example. But every soul has a Torah. To hear another say Torah is a precious gift. For each soul, by the time of his or her final hour, the Torah is complete, the teaching done.

Now God too has a Torah. But God's Torah is beyond lifetimes; it is eternal. And God's Torah is beyond words. It is only the sound of Being itself, the Name of God. As Gershom Scholem observed, "God reveals nothing but God's self ... the name of God... . [Just as] God's language has no grammar; it consists only of names." To read God's Torah then is to hear the Name of Being. Because God's Torah comes from the Self of the Universe into the self of the one who receives, it defies public communication. And what we customarily call the scroll of the Torah is a symbol and reminder in human language that at least we can hear the word of God. God's Torah is infinite meaning. God's Torah is the same as the mystical body of a God who has no body.

Consists only of names Gershom Scholem, "Tradition and Commentary as Religious Categories in Judaism," *Judaism* 15, no. 1 (Winter 1966): 29–30.

All the letters of the Torah, by their shapes, combined and separated, swaddled letters, curved ones and crooked ones, superfluous and elliptic ones, minute and large ones, and inverted, the calligraphy of the letters, the open and closed pericopes and the ordered ones, all of them are the shape of God ... since if one letter is missing from the Scroll of the Torah, or one is superfluous ... that Scroll of the Torah is disqualified, since it has not in itself the shape of God...

The shape of God Moshe Idel, "Infinities of Torah in Kabbalah," in *Midrash and Literature*, ed. Geoffrey H. Hartman and Sanford Budick (New Haven: Yale University Press, 1986), 145.

The *sefer Torah*, the scroll of the Torah, along with the sacred traditions for how to read and interpret it, is the Jewish people's three-millennia-long guess at how to evoke God's Torah with human words. Or, as Rabbi Michael Paley once taught me, "Since God cannot tell pieces of what God knows, God can only tell everything and all at once. For God

Only tell everything in Jerusalem, July 31, 1989.

to tell a piece of what God knows would already be for God to speak in human language."

In this way the scroll of the Torah bears witness to what happened on Mount Sinai, but it is not the content of what happened at Mount Sinai. Or, as Joel Rosenberg once suggested, what we call the Torah is itself only a midrash on some as-yet-undiscovered Ur-text of God's Torah.

God's Torah is creation's master genetic code, the infrastructure of being. God's Torah, in the words of Proverbs, is "a tree of life," the source of each person's self.

A tree of life
Proverbs 3:18.

Ultimately, as our understanding of and devotion to the scroll of the Torah develop, our own individual Torah increasingly comes to resemble God's Torah. Until finally, at the moment of our death, the two become one, our Torah becomes the same as God's Torah. But a person need not wait until his or her final moment. There is one other way. It is called *teshuva*, letting go of one's old self, returning again to one's Source. When we "make" *teshuva* we remember the Source of our innermost selves and our purpose in creation. We are renewed as in the days of old. The old ego slips away and we remember that we are creatures.

The days of old
Lamentations 5:21.

> When you are finally included within *Eyn Sof* [the Holy Nothingness] your Torah is the Torah of God Godself and your prayer is the prayer of God, Godself. There is a Torah of God ... and a prayer of God. When you merit to be included within *Eyn Sof*, your Torah and your prayers are those of God.

The prayer of God
Arthur Green, "Hasidism: Discovery and Retreat," in *The Other Side of God*, ed. Peter L. Berger (New York: Doubleday-Anchor, 1981), 121.

At such moments the unitary Source of all being is revealed to us again. We realize that on our deepest levels what we want and what God wants have been the same all along: our Torah identical with God's. Our desires to behave contrary to God's Torah have been only self-deceptions, contrary to what we really want. This is why they were unsatisfying, unfulfilling, elusive. At our core we want what God wants. The "way" of creation is within us.

Preparation for the study *Itturay Torah,* 6:15.

According to Rabbi Yaakov Yitzhak, the Seer of Lublin, "One needs to make *teshuva* as an act of preparation for the study of Torah." And *teshuva* is nothing less than returning to God.

DREAMING of GOD

"Talk about out-of-body experiences," Jacob mused. "I dreamt I was God. How else to explain that eerie sense of looking down on my sleeping body at the foot of the ladder. There was a sudden, radical, yet effortless and graceful switch in perspective. Instead of looking at the world on the eye level of a sleeping person and of small rodents scurrying about on the desert floor after dark, all at once I beheld everything from a vantage point high above. I saw the mountains and the rocks, the sand and the sky, even the moonlit clouds. And issuing from my body, as if someone had begun to uncoil my DNA molecules into a long strand, was a ladder joining earth and heaven. Its base began with me in heaven and its top reached the earth. And messengers were going down and up on it and at its bottom lies the prostrate body of Jacob, the one destined to be called Israel, the one who, until just a moment ago, I used to be. I want to tell him something. But I cannot seem to get my mouth to utter audible words. (You know how it is in those dreams when you want to shout something but your voice doesn't work.) I shout at the top of my lungs but no sound comes out: 'Wake up Jacob! Don't be afraid. If you want, you can come up the ladder and be one with me right now. The only difference between you and God is you are afraid to realize that we are already the same. Your eyes are my eyes. Open them right now and you will see what I am seeing. Your ears are my ears. Listen now and you will hear my voice issuing from your mouth. Your hands are my hands.' (Oh God, if he would only hear me.) 'This is not a dream, you frightened runaway. I am the God of Abraham and Sarah, Isaac and Rebecca. Do you hear me?' I can see everything. The business with Esau, your mother, your father, everything is happening just the way it is supposed to happen."

EYE of the TEXT

It is not Jacob who says, "God was in this place and I, i did not know." It is you who are reading these words. You are the sacred text itself. The holy text is not about you. You are not even "in" it. You are it.

The words of sacred text reach out to us. The flower wants more than merely to be seen by the eye, it wants to dwell in the eye, to be the eye. The music is not content to be heard by the ear, it wants to live in it, to be the ear. And the silence, that teeming, pulsing noise of all creation, is not content to be beheld by the soul, it is your soul. The sound of the *aleph*, the first letter of the first utterance that has no sound.

What more could Jacob say? Haran was still a long way away, and it wasn't even home.

[183]

Bible Study / Midrash

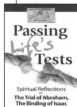

Passing Life's Tests: Spiritual Reflections on the Trial of Abraham, the Binding of Isaac   *By Rabbi Bradley Shavit Artson, DHL*
Invites us to use this powerful tale as a tool for our own soul wrestling, to confront our existential sacrifices and enable us to face—and surmount—life's tests.
6 x 9, 176 pp, Quality PB, 978-1-58023-631-7   **$18.99**

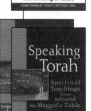

Speaking Torah: Spiritual Teachings from around the Maggid's Table—in Two Volumes   *By Arthur Green, with Ebn Leader, Ariel Evan Mayse and Or N. Rose*
The most powerful Hasidic teachings made accessible—from some of the world's preeminent authorities on Jewish thought and spirituality.
Volume 1—6 x 9, 512 pp, HC, 978-1-58023-668-3   **$34.99**
Volume 2—6 x 9, 448 pp, HC, 978-1-58023-694-2   **$34.99**

A Partner in Holiness: Deepening Mindfulness, Practicing Compassion and Enriching Our Lives through the Wisdom of R. Levi Yitzhak of Berdichev's *Kedushat Levi*
By Rabbi Jonathan P. Slater, DMin; Foreword by Arthur Green; Preface by Rabby Nancy Flam
Contemporary mindfulness and classical Hasidic spirituality are brought together to inspire a satisfying spiritual life of practice.
Volume 1—6 x 9, 336 pp, HC, 978-1-58023-794-9   **$35.00**
Volume 2—6 x 9, 288 pp, HC, 978-1-58023-795-6   **$35.00**

The Genesis of Leadership: What the Bible Teaches Us about Vision, Values and Leading Change   *By Rabbi Nathan Laufer; Foreword by Senator Joseph I. Lieberman*
6 x 9, 288 pp, Quality PB, 978-1-58023-352-1   **$18.99**

Hineini in Our Lives: Learning How to Respond to Others through 14 Biblical Texts and Personal Stories   *By Dr. Norman J. Cohen*   6 x 9, 240 pp, Quality PB, 978-1-58023-274-6   **$18.99**

Masking and Unmasking Ourselves: Interpreting Biblical Texts on Clothing & Identity   *By Dr. Norman J. Cohen*   6 x 9, 224 pp, HC, 978-1-58023-461-0   **$24.99**
Quality PB, 978-1-58023-839-7   **$18.99**

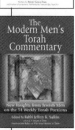

The Messiah and the Jews: Three Thousand Years of Tradition, Belief and Hope
By Rabbi Elaine Rose Glickman; Foreword by Rabbi Neil Gillman, PhD
Preface by Rabbi Judith Z. Abrams, PhD   6 x 9, 192 pp, Quality PB, 978-1-58023-690-4   **$16.99**

The Modern Men's Torah Commentary: New Insights from Jewish Men on the 54 Weekly Torah Portions   *Edited by Rabbi Jeffrey K. Salkin*
6 x 9, 368 pp, HC, 978-1-58023-395-8   **$24.99**

Moses and the Journey to Leadership: Timeless Lessons of Effective Management from the Bible and Today's Leaders   *By Dr. Norman J. Cohen*
6 x 9, 240 pp, Quality PB, 978-1-58023-351-4   **$18.99**; HC, 978-1-58023-227-2   **$21.99**

The Other Talmud—The *Yerushalmi*: Unlocking the Secrets of *The Talmud of Israel* for Judaism Today   *By Rabbi Judith Z. Abrams, PhD*
6 x 9, 256 pp, HC, 978-1-58023-463-4   **$24.99**

Sage Tales: Wisdom and Wonder from the Rabbis of the Talmud
By Rabbi Burton L. Visotzky
6 x 9, 256 pp, Quality PB, 978-1-58023-791-8   **$19.99**; HC, 978-1-58023-456-6   **$24.99**

The Torah Revolution: Fourteen Truths That Changed the World
By Rabbi Reuven Hammer, PhD   6 x 9, 240 pp, Quality PB, 978-1-58023-789-5   **$18.99**
HC, 978-1-58023-457-3   **$24.99**

The Wisdom of Judaism: An Introduction to the Values of the Talmud
By Rabbi Dov Peretz Elkins   6 x 9, 192 pp, Quality PB, 978-1-58023-327-9   **$16.99**

Or phone, fax, mail or email to: **JEWISH LIGHTS Publishing**
Sunset Farm Offices, Route 4 • P.O. Box 237 • Woodstock, Vermont 05091
Tel: (802) 457-4000 • Fax: (802) 457-4004 • www.jewishlights.com
Credit card orders: **(800) 962-4544** (8:30AM–5:30PM EST Monday–Friday)
Generous discounts on quantity orders. SATISFACTION GUARANTEED. Prices subject to change.

Social Justice

Where Justice Dwells
A Hands-On Guide to Doing Social Justice in Your Jewish Community
By Rabbi Jill Jacobs; Foreword by Rabbi David Saperstein
Provides ways to envision and act on your own ideals of social justice.
7 x 9, 288 pp, Quality PB, 978-1-58023-453-5 **$24.99**

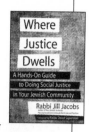

There Shall Be No Needy
Pursuing Social Justice through Jewish Law and Tradition
By Rabbi Jill Jacobs; Foreword by Rabbi Elliot N. Dorff, PhD; Preface by Simon Greer
Confronts the most pressing issues of twenty-first-century America from a deeply
Jewish perspective. 6 x 9, 288 pp, Quality PB, 978-1-58023-425-2 **$16.99**
There Shall Be No Needy Teacher's Guide 8½ x 11, 56 pp, PB, 978-1-58023-429-0 **$8.99**

Conscience
The Duty to Obey and the Duty to Disobey
By Rabbi Harold M. Schulweis (z"l)
Examines the idea of conscience and the role conscience plays in our relationships
to government, law, ethics, religion, human nature, God—and to each other.
6 x 9, 160 pp, Quality PB, 978-1-58023-419-1 **$16.99**; HC, 978-1-58023-375-0 **$19.99**

Judaism and Justice: The Jewish Passion to Repair the World
By Rabbi Sidney Schwarz; Foreword by Ruth Messinger
6 x 9, 352 pp, Quality PB, 978-1-58023-353-8 **$19.99**

Spirituality / Women's Interest

Embracing the Divine Feminine: Finding God through the Ecstasy of
Physical Love—The Song of Songs Annotated & Explained
Annotation and Translation by Rabbi Rami Shapiro; Foreword by Rev. Cynthia Bourgeault, PhD
Restores the Song of Songs' eroticism and interprets it as a celebration of the love
between the Divine Feminine and the contemporary spiritual seeker.
5½ x 8½, 176 pp, Quality PB, 978-1-59473-575-2 **$16.99***

The Women's Haftarah Commentary
New Insights from Women Rabbis on the 54 Weekly Haftarah Portions,
the 5 Megillot & Special Shabbatot
Edited by Rabbi Elyse Goldstein
Illuminates the historical significance of female portrayals in the Haftarah and the
Five Megillot. 6 x 9, 560 pp, Quality PB, 978-1-58023-371-2 **$19.99**

The Women's Torah Commentary
New Insights from Women Rabbis on the 54 Weekly Torah Portions
Edited by Rabbi Elyse Goldstein
Over fifty women rabbis offer inspiring insights on the Torah, in a week-by-week format.
6 x 9, 496 pp, Quality PB, 978-1-58023-370-5 **$19.99**

The Divine Feminine in Biblical Wisdom Literature
Selections Annotated & Explained
Translation & Annotation by Rabbi Rami Shapiro; Foreword by Rev. Cynthia Bourgeault, PhD
5½ x 8½, 240 pp, Quality PB, 978-1-59473-109-9 **$18.99***

New Jewish Feminism: Probing the Past, Forging the Future
Edited by Rabbi Elyse Goldstein; Foreword by Anita Diamant
6 x 9, 480 pp, HC, 978-1-58023-359-0 **$24.99**

The Quotable Jewish Woman
Wisdom, Inspiration & Humor from the Mind & Heart
Edited by Elaine Bernstein Partnow
6 x 9, 496 pp, Quality PB, 978-1-58023-236-4 **$19.99**

See Passover for *The Women's Passover Companion: Women's Reflections on
the Festival of Freedom* and *The Women's Seder Sourcebook: Rituals &
Readings for Use at the Passover Seder.*

*A book from SkyLight Paths, Jewish Lights' sister imprint

Theology / Philosophy / The Way Into... Series

The Way Into... series offers an accessible and highly usable "guided tour" of the Jewish faith, people, history and beliefs—in total, an introduction to Judaism that will enable you to understand and interact with the sacred texts of the Jewish tradition. Each volume is written by a leading contemporary scholar and teacher, and explores one key aspect of Judaism. The Way Into... series enables all readers to achieve a real sense of Jewish cultural literacy through guided study.

The Way Into Encountering God in Judaism
By Rabbi Neil Gillman, PhD
For everyone who wants to understand how Jews have encountered God throughout history and today.
6 x 9, 240 pp, Quality PB, 978-1-58023-199-2 **$18.99**; HC, 978-1-58023-025-4 **$21.95**
Also Available: **The Jewish Approach to God:** A Brief Introduction for Christians
By Rabbi Neil Gillman, PhD
5½ x 8½, 192 pp, Quality PB, 978-1-58023-190-9 **$18.99**

The Way Into Jewish Mystical Tradition
By Rabbi Lawrence Kushner
Allows readers to interact directly with the sacred mystical texts of the Jewish tradition. An accessible introduction to the concepts of Jewish mysticism, their religious and spiritual significance, and how they relate to life today.
6 x 9, 224 pp, Quality PB, 978-1-58023-200-5 **$18.99**

The Way Into Jewish Prayer
By Rabbi Lawrence A. Hoffman, PhD
Opens the door to 3,000 years of Jewish prayer, making anyone feel at home in the Jewish way of communicating with God.
6 x 9, 208 pp, Quality PB, 978-1-58023-201-2 **$18.99**

The Way Into Jewish Prayer Teacher's Guide
By Rabbi Jennifer Ossakow Goldsmith
8½ x 11, 42 pp, PB, 978-1-58023-345-3 **$8.99**
Download a free copy at www.jewishlights.com.

The Way Into Judaism and the Environment
By Jeremy Benstein, PhD
Explores the ways in which Judaism contributes to contemporary social-environmental issues, the extent to which Judaism is part of the problem and how it can be part of the solution.
6 x 9, 288 pp, Quality PB, 978-1-58023-368-2 **$18.99**; HC, 978-1-58023-268-5 **$24.99**

The Way Into *Tikkun Olam* (Repairing the World)
By Rabbi Elliot N. Dorff, PhD
An accessible introduction to the Jewish concept of the individual's responsibility to care for others and repair the world.
6 x 9, 304 pp, Quality PB, 978-1-58023-328-6 **$18.99**

The Way Into Torah
By Rabbi Norman J. Cohen, PhD
Helps guide you in the exploration of the origins and development of Torah, explains why it should be studied and how to do it.
6 x 9, 176 pp, Quality PB, 978-1-58023-198-5 **$16.99**

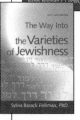

The Way Into the Varieties of Jewishness
By Sylvia Barack Fishman, PhD
Explores the religious and historical understanding of what it has meant to be Jewish from ancient times to the present controversy over "Who is a Jew?"
6 x 9, 288 pp, Quality PB, 978-1-58023-367-5 **$18.99**; HC, 978-1-58023-030-8 **$24.99**

Theology / Philosophy

Renewing the Process of Creation: A Jewish Integration of Science and Spirit *By Rabbi Bradley Shavit Artson, DHL*
A daring blend of Jewish theology, science and Process Thought, exploring personal actions through Judaism and the sciences as dynamically interactive and mutually informative.   6 x 9, 208 pp, HC, 978-1-58023-833-5 **$24.99**

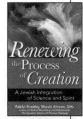

Does the Soul Survive? 2nd Edition: A Jewish Journey to Belief in Afterlife, Past Lives & Living with Purpose *By Rabbi Elie Kaplan Spitz*
Foreword by Brian L. Weiss, MD A skeptic turned believer recounts his quest to uncover the Jewish tradition's answers about what happens to our souls after death.
6 x 9, 288 pp, Quality PB, 978-1-58023-818-2 **$18.99**

God of Becoming and Relationship: The Dynamic Nature of Process Theology *By Rabbi Bradley Shavit Artson, DHL* Explains how Process Theology breaks us free from the strictures of ancient Greek and medieval European philosophy.   6 x 9, 208 pp, HC, 978-1-58023-713-0 **$24.99**

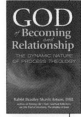

The Way of Man: According to Hasidic Teaching
By Martin Buber; New Translation and Introduction by Rabbi Bernard H. Mehlman and Dr. Gabriel E. Padawer; Foreword by Paul Mendes-Flohr
An accessible and engaging new translation of Buber's classic work—*available as an eBook only.* eBook, 978-1-58023-601-0 **$18.99**

Believing and Its Tensions: A Personal Conversation about God, Torah, Suffering and Death in Jewish Thought *By Rabbi Neil Gillman, PhD*
5½ x 8½, 144 pp, HC, 978-1-58023-669-0 **$19.99**

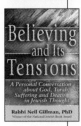

The Death of Death: Resurrection and Immortality in Jewish Thought
By Rabbi Neil Gillman, PhD   6 x 9, 336 pp, Quality PB, 978-1-58023-081-0 **$19.99**

From Defender to Critic: The Search for a New Jewish Self
By Dr. David Hartman (z"l)   6 x 9, 336 pp, HC, 978-1-58023-515-0 **$35.00**

The God Who Hates Lies: Confronting & Rethinking Jewish Tradition
By Dr. David Hartman (z"l) with Charlie Buckholtz 6 x 9, 208 pp, Quality PB, 978-1-58023-790-1 **$19.99**

A Heart of Many Rooms: Celebrating the Many Voices within Judaism
By Dr. David Hartman (z"l)   6 x 9, 352 pp, Quality PB, 978-1-58023-156-5 **$24.99**

Jewish Theology in Our Time: A New Generation Explores the Foundations and Future of Jewish Belief *Edited by Rabbi Elliot J. Cosgrove, PhD; Foreword by Rabbi David J. Wolpe*
Preface by Rabbi Carole B. Balin, PhD
6 x 9, 240 pp, Quality PB, 978-1-58023-630-0 **$19.99**; HC, 978-1-58023-413-9 **$24.99**

Maimonides—Essential Teachings on Jewish Faith & Ethics: The Book of Knowledge & the Thirteen Principles of Faith—Annotated & Explained
Translation and Annotation by Rabbi Marc D. Angel, PhD
5½ x 8½, 224 pp, Quality PB, 978-1-59473-311-6 **$18.99***

Our Religious Brains: What Cognitive Science Reveals about Belief, Mortality, Community and Our Relationship with God *By Rabbi Ralph D. Mecklenburger;*
Foreword by Dr. Howard Kelfer; Preface by Dr. Neil Gillman
6 x 9, 224 pp, HC, 978-1-58023-508-2 **$24.99**; Quality PB, 978-1-58023-840-3 **$18.99**

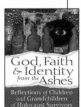

God, Faith & Identity from the Ashes
Reflections of Children and Grandchildren of Holocaust Survivors
Almost ninety contributors from sixteen countries inform, challenge and inspire people of all backgrounds.   *Edited by Menachem Z. Rosensaft; Prologue by Elie Wiesel*
6 x 9, 352 pp, HC, 978-1-58023-805-2 **$25.00**

I Am Jewish
Personal Reflections Inspired by the Last Words of Daniel Pearl
Almost 150 Jews—both famous and not—from all walks of life, from all around the world, write about many aspects of their Judaism.
Edited by Judea and Ruth Pearl 6 x 9, 304 pp, Deluxe PB w/ flaps, 978-1-58023-259-3 **$19.99**
Download a free copy of the *I Am Jewish Teacher's Guide* at www.jewishlights.com.

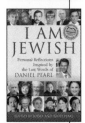

*A book from SkyLight Paths, Jewish Lights' sister imprint

Meditation / Yoga

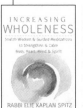

Increasing Wholeness: Jewish Wisdom & Guided Meditations to Strengthen & Calm Body, Heart, Mind & Spirit
By Rabbi Elie Kaplan Spitz Combines Jewish tradition, contemporary psychology and world spiritual writings with practical contemplative exercises to guide you to see the familiar in fresh new ways.
6 x 9, 208 pp, Quality PB, 978-1-58023-823-6 **$19.99**

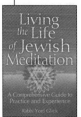

Living the Life of Jewish Meditation: A Comprehensive Guide to Practice and Experience *By Rabbi Yoel Glick*
Combines the knowledge of Judaism with the spiritual practice of Yoga to lead you to an encounter with your true self. Includes nineteen different meditations.
6 x 9, 272 pp, Quality PB, 978-1-58023-802-1 **$18.99**

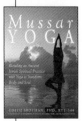

Mussar Yoga: Blending an Ancient Jewish Spiritual Practice with Yoga to Transform Body and Soul
By Edith R. Brotman, PhD, RYT-500; Foreword by Alan Morinis
A clear and easy-to-use introduction to an embodied spiritual practice for anyone seeking profound and lasting self-transformation.
7 x 9, 224 pp, 40+ b/w photos, Quality PB, 978-1-58023-784-0 **$18.99**

The Magic of Hebrew Chant: Healing the Spirit, Transforming the Mind, Deepening Love *By Rabbi Shefa Gold; Foreword by Sylvia Boorstein*
Introduces this transformative spiritual practice as a way to unlock the power of sacred texts and make prayer and meditation the delight of your life. Includes musical notations.   6 x 9, 352 pp, Quality PB, 978-1-58023-671-3 **$24.99**

The Magic of Hebrew Chant Companion—The Big Book of Musical Notations and Incantations   8½ x 11, 154 pp, PB, 978-1-58023-722-2 **$19.99**

Aleph-Bet Yoga: Embodying the Hebrew Letters for Physical and Spiritual Well-Being
By Steven A. Rapp; Foreword by Tamar Frankiel, PhD, and Judy Greenfeld; Preface by Hart Lazer
7 x 10, 128 pp, b/w photos, Quality PB, Lay-flat binding, 978-1-58023-162-6 **$16.95**

Discovering Jewish Meditation, 2nd Edition
Instruction & Guidance for Learning an Ancient Spiritual Practice
By Nan Fink Gefen, PhD   6 x 9, 208 pp, Quality PB, 978-1-58023-462-7 **$16.99**

The Handbook of Jewish Meditation Practices
A Guide for Enriching the Sabbath and Other Days of Your Life
By Rabbi David A. Cooper 6 x 9, 208 pp, Quality PB, 978-1-58023-102-2 **$16.95**

Jewish Meditation Practices for Everyday Life: Awakening Your Heart, Connecting with God *By Rabbi Jeff Roth* 6 x 9, 224 pp, Quality PB, 978-1-58023-397-2 **$18.99**

Ritual / Sacred Practices

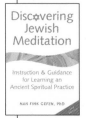

God in Your Body: Kabbalah, Mindfulness and Embodied Spiritual Practice
By Jay Michaelson 6 x 9, 272 pp, Quality PB, 978-1-58023-304-0 **$18.99**

Jewish Ritual: A Brief Introduction for Christians
By Rabbi Kerry M. Olitzky and Rabbi Daniel Judson
5½ x 8½, 144 pp, Quality PB, 978-1-58023-210-4 **$14.99**

The Rituals & Practices of a Jewish Life: A Handbook for Personal Spiritual Renewal
Edited by Rabbi Kerry M. Olitzky and Rabbi Daniel Judson
6 x 9, 272 pp, Illus., Quality PB, 978-1-58023-169-5 **$19.99**

The Sacred Art of Lovingkindness: Preparing to Practice
By Rabbi Rami Shapiro 5½ x 8½, 176 pp, Quality PB, 978-1-59473-151-8 **$16.99***

Mystery & Detective Fiction

Criminal Kabbalah: An Intriguing Anthology of Jewish Mystery & Detective Fiction
Edited by Lawrence W. Raphael; Foreword by Laurie R. King
6 x 9, 256 pp, Quality PB, 978-1-58023-109-1 **$16.95**

Mystery Midrash: An Anthology of Jewish Mystery & Detective Fiction
Edited by Lawrence W. Raphael; Preface by Joel Siegel
6 x 9, 304 pp, Quality PB, 978-1-58023-055-1 **$16.95**

*A book from SkyLight Paths, Jewish Lights' sister imprint

Kabbalah / Mysticism

Walking the Path of the Jewish Mystic
How to Expand Your Awareness and Transform Your Life   *By Rabbi Yoel Glick*
A unique guide to the nature of both physical and spiritual reality.
6 x 9, 224 pp, Quality PB, 978-1-58023-843-4   **$18.99**

Ehyeh: A Kabbalah for Tomorrow
By Rabbi Arthur Green, PhD   6 x 9, 224 pp, Quality PB, 978-1-58023-213-5   **$18.99**

The Gift of Kabbalah: Discovering the Secrets of Heaven, Renewing Your Life on Earth
By Tamar Frankiel, PhD   6 x 9, 256 pp, Quality PB, 978-1-58023-141-1   **$18.99**

Jewish Mysticism and the Spiritual Life: Classical Texts, Contemporary
Reflections   *Edited by Dr. Lawrence Fine, Dr. Eitan Fishbane and Rabbi Or N. Rose*
6 x 9, 256 pp, Quality PB, 978-1-58023-719-2   **$18.99**

Seek My Face: A Jewish Mystical Theology   *By Rabbi Arthur Green, PhD*
6 x 9, 304 pp, Quality PB, 978-1-58023-130-5   **$19.95**

Zohar: Annotated & Explained   *Translation & Annotation by Dr. Daniel C. Matt*
Foreword by Andrew Harvey   5½ x 8½, 176 pp, Quality PB, 978-1-893361-51-5   **$18.99**
(A book from SkyLight Paths, Jewish Lights' sister imprint)

See also *The Way Into Jewish Mystical Tradition* in The Way Into... Series

Inspiration

The Best Boy in the United States of America
A Memoir of Blessings and Kisses   *By Dr. Ron Wolfson*
Will resonate with anyone seeking to shape stronger families and communities
and live a life of joy and purpose.   6 x 9, 192 pp, HC, 978-1-58023-838-0   **$19.99**

The Chutzpah Imperative: Empowering Today's Jews for a Life
That Matters   *By Rabbi Edward Feinstein; Foreword by Rabbi Laura Geller*
A new view of chutzpah as Jewish self-empowerment to be God's partner and
repair the world. Reveals Judaism's ancient message, its deepest purpose and most
precious treasures.   6 x 9, 192 pp, HC, 978-1-58023-792-5   **$21.99**

Judaism's Ten Best Ideas: A Brief Guide for Seekers
By Rabbi Arthur Green, PhD   A highly accessible introduction to Judaism's greatest
contributions to civilization, drawing on Jewish mystical tradition and the author's
experience.   4½ x 6½, 112 pp, Quality PB, 978-1-58023-803-8   **$9.99**

The Empty Chair: Finding Hope and Joy—Timeless Wisdom from a Hasidic Master,
Rebbe Nachman of Breslov   *Adapted by Moshe Mykoff and the Breslov Research Institute*
4 x 6, 128 pp, Deluxe PB w/ flaps, 978-1-879045-67-5   **$9.99**

The Gentle Weapon: Prayers for Everyday and Not-So-Everyday Moments—
Timeless Wisdom from the Teachings of the Hasidic Master Rebbe Nachman of Breslov
Adapted by Moshe Mykoff and S. C. Mizrahi, together with the Breslov Research Institute
4 x 6, 144 pp, Deluxe PB w/ flaps, 978-1-58023-022-3   **$9.99**

God Whispers: Stories of the Soul, Lessons of the Heart   *By Rabbi Karyn D. Kedar*
6 x 9, 176 pp, Quality PB, 978-1-58023-088-9   **$16.99**

God's To-Do List: 103 Ways to Be an Angel and Do God's Work on Earth
By Dr. Ron Wolfson   6 x 9, 144 pp, Quality PB, 978-1-58023-301-9   **$16.99**

Happiness and the Human Spirit: The Spirituality of Becoming the Best You Can Be
By Rabbi Abraham J. Twerski, MD
6 x 9, 176 pp, Quality PB, 978-1-58023-404-7   **$16.99**; HC, 978-1-58023-343-9   **$19.99**

Life's Daily Blessings: Inspiring Reflections on Gratitude and Joy for Every Day,
Based on Jewish Wisdom   *By Rabbi Kerry M. Olitzky*
4½ x 6½, 368 pp, Quality PB, 978-1-58023-396-5   **$16.99**

Sacred Intentions: Morning Inspiration to Strengthen the Spirit, Based on Jewish Wisdom
By Rabbi Kerry M. Olitzky and Rabbi Lori Forman-Jacobi
4½ x 6½, 448 pp, Quality PB, 978-1-58023-061-2   **$16.99**

The Seven Questions You're Asked in Heaven: Reviewing and Renewing Your
Life on Earth   *By Dr. Ron Wolfson*   6 x 9, 176 pp, Quality PB, 978-1-58023-407-8   **$16.99**

Spirituality

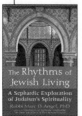

The Rhythms of Jewish Living
A Sephardic Exploration of Judaism's Spirituality
By Rabbi Marc D. Angel, PhD Reclaims the natural, balanced and insightful teachings of Sephardic Judaism that can and should imbue modern Jewish spirituality.
6 x 9, 208 pp, Quality PB, 978-1-58023-834-2 **$18.99**

God and the Big Bang, 2nd Edition
Discovering Harmony between Science and Spirituality
By Daniel C. Matt Updated and expanded. Draws on the insights of physics and Kabbalah to uncover the sense of wonder and oneness that connects humankind with the universe and God. 6 x 9, 224 pp (est), Quality PB, 978-1-58023-836-6 **$18.99**

Amazing Chesed: Living a Grace-Filled Judaism
By Rabbi Rami Shapiro Drawing from ancient and contemporary, traditional and non-traditional Jewish wisdom, reclaims the idea of grace in Judaism.
6 x 9, 176 pp, Quality PB, 978-1-58023-624-9 **$16.99**

Perennial Wisdom for the Spiritually Independent: Sacred Teachings—
Annotated & Explained Annotation by Rabbi Rami Shapiro; Foreword by Richard Rohr
Weaves sacred texts and teachings from the world's major religions into a coherent exploration of the five core questions at the heart of every religion's search.
5½ x 8½, 336 pp, Quality PB, 978-1-59473-515-8 **$16.99***

A Book of Life: Embracing Judaism as a Spiritual Practice
By Rabbi Michael Strassfeld 6 x 9, 544 pp, Quality PB, 978-1-58023-247-0 **$24.99**

Bringing the Psalms to Life: How to Understand and Use the Book of Psalms
By Rabbi Daniel F. Polish, PhD 6 x 9, 208 pp, Quality PB, 978-1-58023-157-2 **$18.99**

Does the Soul Survive? 2nd Edition: A Jewish Journey to Belief in Afterlife, Past Lives
& Living with Purpose By Rabbi Elie Kaplan Spitz; Foreword by Brian L. Weiss, MD
6 x 9, 288 pp, Quality PB, 978-1-58023-818-2 **$18.99**

First Steps to a New Jewish Spirit: Reb Zalman's Guide to Recapturing the Intimacy &
Ecstasy in Your Relationship with God By Rabbi Zalman Schachter-Shalomi (z"l) with Donald Gropman
6 x 9, 144 pp, Quality PB, 978-1-58023-182-4 **$16.95**

Foundations of Sephardic Spirituality: The Inner Life of Jews of the Ottoman Empire
By Rabbi Marc D. Angel, PhD 6 x 9, 224 pp, Quality PB, 978-1-58023-341-5 **$18.99**

The God Upgrade: Finding Your 21st-Century Spirituality in Judaism's 5,000-Year-
Old Tradition By Rabbi Jamie Korngold; Foreword by Rabbi Harold M. Schulweis
6 x 9, 176 pp, Quality PB, 978-1-58023-443-6 **$15.99**

The Jewish Lights Spirituality Handbook: A Guide to Understanding, Exploring &
Living a Spiritual Life Edited by Stuart M. Matlins
6 x 9, 456 pp, Quality PB, 978-1-58023-093-3 **$19.99**

Jewish with Feeling: A Guide to Meaningful Jewish Practice
By Rabbi Zalman Schachter-Shalomi (z"l) with Joel Segel
5½ x 8½, 288 pp, Quality PB, 978-1-58023-691-1 **$19.99**

Judaism, Physics and God: Searching for Sacred Metaphors in a Post-Einstein World
By Rabbi David W. Nelson
6 x 9, 352 pp, Quality PB, inc. reader's discussion guide, 978-1-58023-306-4 **$18.99**
HC, 352 pp, 978-1-58023-252-4 **$24.99**

Repentance: The Meaning and Practice of Teshuvah
By Dr. Louis E. Newman; Foreword by Rabbi Harold M. Schulweis; Preface by Rabbi Karyn D. Kedar
6 x 9, 256 pp, Quality PB, 978-1-58023-718-5 **$18.99**

Tanya, the Masterpiece of Hasidic Wisdom: Selections Annotated & Explained
Translation & Annotation by Rabbi Rami Shapiro; Foreword by Rabbi Zalman Schachter-Shalomi (z"l)
5½ x 8½, 240 pp, Quality PB, 978-1-59473-275-1 **$18.99***

These Are the Words, 2nd Edition: A Vocabulary of Jewish Spiritual Life
By Rabbi Arthur Green, PhD 6 x 9, 320 pp, Quality PB, 978-1-58023-494-8 **$19.99**

Your Word Is Fire: The Hasidic Masters on Contemplative Prayer
Edited and translated by Rabbi Arthur Green, PhD, and Barry W. Holtz
6 x 9, 160 pp, Quality PB, 978-1-879045-25-5 **$16.99**

*A book from SkyLight Paths, Jewish Lights' sister imprint

Spirituality / Prayer

Davening: A Guide to Meaningful Jewish Prayer
By Rabbi Zalman Schachter-Shalomi (z"l) with Joel Segel; Foreword by Rabbi Lawrence Kushner
A fresh approach to prayer for all who wish to appreciate the power of prayer's poetry, song and ritual, and to join the age-old conversation that Jews have had with God. 6 x 9, 240 pp, Quality PB, 978-1-58023-627-0 **$18.99**

Jewish Men Pray: Words of Yearning, Praise, Petition, Gratitude and Wonder from Traditional and Contemporary Sources
Edited by Rabbi Kerry M. Olitzky and Stuart M. Matlins; Foreword by Rabbi Bradley Shavit Artson, DHL
A celebration of Jewish men's voices in prayer—to strengthen, heal, comfort, and inspire—from the ancient world up to our own day.
5 x 7¼, 400 pp, HC, 978-1-58023-628-7 **$19.99**

Making Prayer Real: Leading Jewish Spiritual Voices on Why Prayer Is Difficult and What to Do about It *By Rabbi Mike Comins* 6 x 9, 320 pp, Quality PB, 978-1-58023-417-7 **$18.99**

Witnesses to the One: The Spiritual History of the *Sh'ma*
By Rabbi Joseph B. Meszler; Foreword by Rabbi Elyse Goldstein
6 x 9, 176 pp, Quality PB, 978-1-58023-400-9 **$16.99**; HC, 978-1-58023-309-5 **$19.99**

My People's Prayer Book Series: Traditional Prayers, Modern Commentaries *Edited by Rabbi Lawrence A. Hoffman, PhD*
Provides diverse and exciting commentary to the traditional liturgy. Will help you find new wisdom in Jewish prayer, and bring liturgy into your life. Each book includes Hebrew text, modern translations and commentaries from all perspectives of the Jewish world.

Vol. 1—The *Sh'ma* and Its Blessings
  7 x 10, 168 pp, HC, 978-1-879045-79-8 **$29.99**
Vol. 2—The *Amidah* 7 x 10, 240 pp, HC, 978-1-879045-80-4 **$29.99**
Vol. 3—*P'sukei D'zimrah* (Morning Psalms)
  7 x 10, 240 pp, HC, 978-1-879045-81-1 **$35.00**
Vol. 4—*Seder K'riat Hatorah* (The Torah Service)
  7 x 10, 264 pp, HC, 978-1-879045-82-8 **$29.99**
Vol. 5—*Birkhot Hashachar* (Morning Blessings)
  7 x 10, 240 pp, HC, 978-1-879045-83-5 **$35.00**
Vol. 6—*Tachanun* and Concluding Prayers
  7 x 10, 240 pp, HC, 978-1-879045-84-2 **$24.95**
Vol. 7—*Shabbat at Home* 7 x 10, 240 pp, HC, 978-1-879045-85-9 **$29.99**
Vol. 8—*Kabbalat Shabbat* (Welcoming Shabbat in the Synagogue)
  7 x 10, 240 pp, HC, 978-1-58023-121-3 **$24.99**
Vol. 9—*Welcoming the Night: Minchah* and *Ma'ariv* (Afternoon and Evening Prayer) 7 x 10, 272 pp, HC, 978-1-58023-262-3 **$35.00**
Vol. 10—*Shabbat Morning: Shacharit* and *Musaf* (Morning and Additional Services) 7 x 10, 240 pp, HC, 978-1-58023-240-1 **$35.00**

Spirituality / Lawrence Kushner

I'm God; You're Not: Observations on Organized Religion & Other Disguises of the Ego
6 x 9, 256 pp, Quality PB, 978-1-58023-513-6 **$18.99**; HC, 978-1-58023-441-2 **$21.99**

The Book of Letters: A Mystical Hebrew Alphabet
Popular HC Edition, 6 x 9, 80 pp, 2-color text, 978-1-879045-00-2 **$24.95**
Collector's Limited Edition, 9 x 12, 80 pp, gold-foil-embossed pages, w/ limited-edition silk-screened print, 978-1-879045-04-0 **$349.00**

The Book of Miracles: A Young Person's Guide to Jewish Spiritual Awareness
6 x 9, 96 pp, 2-color illus., HC, 978-1-879045-78-1 **$16.95** *For ages 9–13*

God Was in This Place & I, i Did Not Know: Finding Self, Spirituality and Ultimate Meaning 6 x 9, 192 pp, Quality PB, 978-1-879045-33-0 **$18.99**

Honey from the Rock: An Introduction to Jewish Mysticism
6 x 9, 176 pp, Quality PB, 978-1-58023-073-5 **$18.99**

Invisible Lines of Connection: Sacred Stories of the Ordinary
5½ x 8½, 160 pp, Quality PB, 978-1-879045-98-9 **$16.99**

The Way Into Jewish Mystical Tradition
6 x 9, 224 pp, Quality PB, 978-1-58023-200-5 **$18.99**

About Jewish Lights

People of all faiths and backgrounds yearn for books that attract, engage, educate, and spiritually inspire.

Our principal goal is to stimulate thought and help all people learn about who the Jewish People are, where they come from, and what the future can be made to hold. While people of our diverse Jewish heritage are the primary audience, our books speak to people in the Christian world as well and will broaden their understanding of Judaism and the roots of their own faith.

We bring to you authors who are at the forefront of spiritual thought and experience. While each has something different to say, they all say it in a voice that you can hear.

Our books are designed to welcome you and then to engage, stimulate, and inspire. We judge our success not only by whether or not our books are beautiful and commercially successful, but by whether or not they make a difference in your life.

For your information and convenience, at the back of this book we have provided a list of other Jewish Lights books you might find interesting and useful. They cover all the categories of your life:

Bar/Bat Mitzvah
Bible Study / Midrash
Children's Books
Congregation Resources
Current Events / History
Ecology / Environment
Fiction: Mystery, Science Fiction
Grief / Healing
Holidays / Holy Days
Inspiration
Kabbalah / Mysticism / Enneagram

Life Cycle
Meditation
Men's Interest
Parenting
Prayer / Ritual / Sacred Practice
Social Justice
Spirituality
Theology / Philosophy
Travel
Twelve Steps
Women's Interest

Stuart M. Matlins, Publisher

Or phone, fax, mail or email to: **JEWISH LIGHTS Publishing**
Sunset Farm Offices, Route 4 • P.O. Box 237 • Woodstock, Vermont 05091
Tel: (802) 457-4000 • Fax: (802) 457-4004 • www.jewishlights.com
Credit card orders: **(800) 962-4544** (8:30AM–5:30PM EST Monday–Friday)
Generous discounts on quantity orders. SATISFACTION GUARANTEED. Prices subject to change.